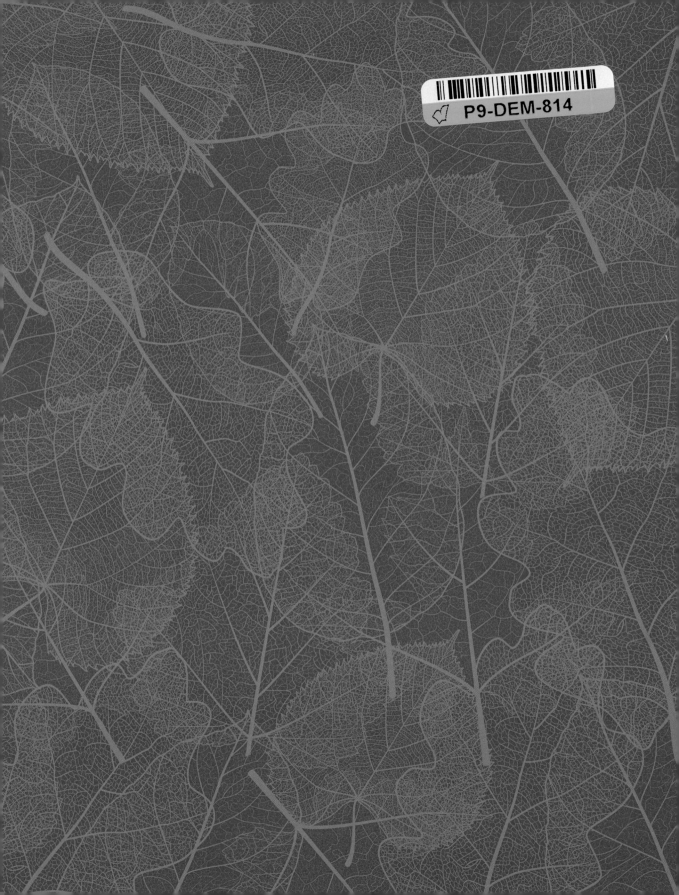

60-SECOND GENIUS

PLANET EARTH

WELBECK

Published in 2021 by Welbeck Children's Books

An imprint of Welbeck Children's Limited, part of
Welbeck Publishing Group
20 Mortimer Street London W1T 3JW

ISBN 978 1 78312 723 8
Printed in Dongguan, China
10 9 8 7 6 5 4 3 2 1

Author: Jon Richards
Text and design: Tall Tree Ltd.
Editorial Manager: Joff Brown
Design Manager: Sam James
Production: Melanie Robertson

60-SECOND GENIUS

PLANET EARTH

BITE-SIZE FACTS TO MAKE LEARNING FUN AND FAST

JON RICHARDS

CONTENTS

CHAPTER 1

FORMATION
AND STRUCTURE

CHAPTER 2

CHANGING
PLANET

CHAPTER 3

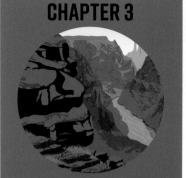

ROCKS AND
MINERALS

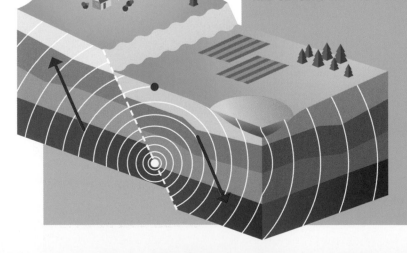

CHAPTER 4

BLUE
PLANET

CHAPTER 5

THE
ATMOSPHERE

CHAPTER 6

LIVING
PLANET

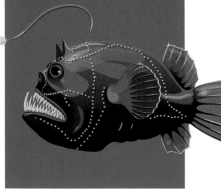

PLANET EARTH

Since it was formed about 4.5 billion years ago, Earth has developed into an amazing world. It's surface is forever changing as powerful forces inside the planet pull and push on the crust above, building mountains, tearing apart continents and constructing whole new pieces of land.

Surrounding it is an atmosphere of gasses, which provides organisms with life-giving oxygen and produces our weather (with a little help from the Sun).

Our planet may appear large, but it is still quite fragile. Changes to our climate over the last 150 years have threatened many habitats around the world, endangering the species living there and bringing many of them to the verge of extinction.

CHAPTER 1

FORMATION
AND STRUCTURE

SOLAR FAMILY

Earth is part of a large family of planets, dwarf planets, comets, and other rocky bodies that all orbit around a ball of burning gas, the Sun.

The Sun
Although it is a yellow dwarf star and small compared to other stars in the Milky Way, the Sun is the largest object in the Solar System. It accounts for about 99.8 per cent of the Solar System's mass.

Rocky planets
The four inner planets, Mercury, Venus, Earth, and Mars, are comparatively small and made mainly from rock. Only two of these, Earth and Mars, have their own natural satellites, or moons. Earth has one moon, while Mars has two.

Mercury

Venus

Earth

Mars

Gas giants and ice giants
The four outermost planets are large balls of gas and ice. Jupiter and Saturn are known as gas giants because they are made up mainly from different gases, while Uranus and Neptune are called ice giants, because they are made up of ice. All four of these have rings and they have more than 200 moons between them.

Jupiter

Neptune

Saturn

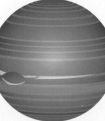

Uranus

Earth is one of eight planets and millions of pieces of rock and ice that orbit the Sun. These objects formed about 4.5 billion years ago.

From the start

Scientists divide the age of Earth into different lengths of time, with the longest intervals divided into smaller and smaller sub-divisions. These are (from longest to shortest) eons, eras, periods, epochs, and ages.

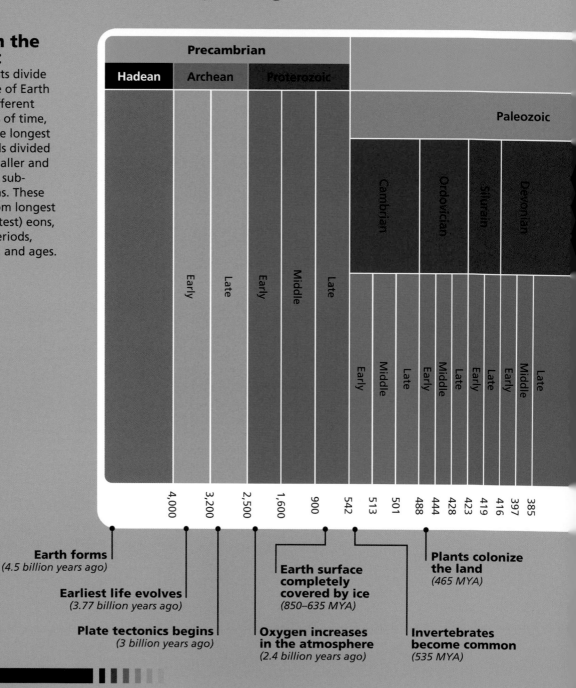

Earth forms
(4.5 billion years ago)

Earliest life evolves
(3.77 billion years ago)

Plate tectonics begins
(3 billion years ago)

Oxygen increases in the atmosphere
(2.4 billion years ago)

Earth surface completely covered by ice
(850–635 MYA)

Invertebrates become common
(535 MYA)

Plants colonize the land
(465 MYA)

Some of the oldest rocks discovered on Earth are the Acasta Gneiss that are

4.03 billion years old

and were found near the Great Slave Lake in northwest Canada.

How do we know Earth's age?

Scientists have calculated how old Earth is by dating rocks in Earth's crust and in rock samples from other bodies in the Solar System, such as the Moon, asteroids, and meteorites that crash into Earth's surface.

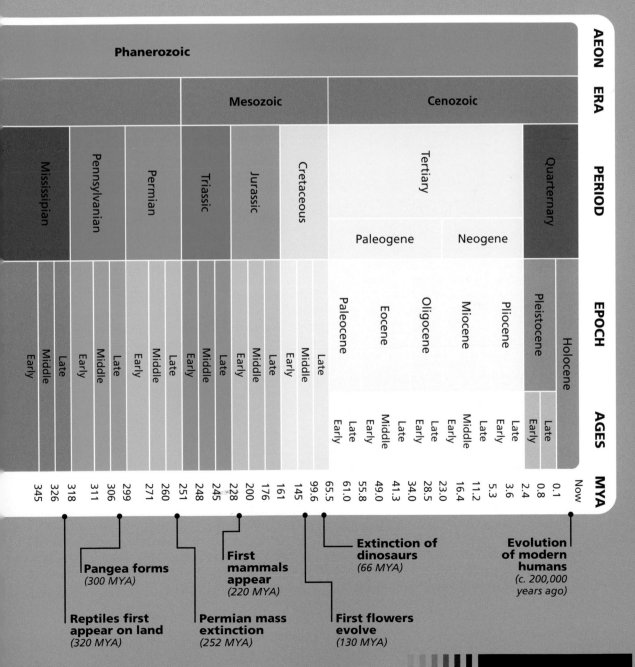

More than 4.5 billion years ago, the Solar System was a swirling disc of gas, dust, and rocks orbiting around a clump of matter that was to become the Sun.

1. The Sun ignites

Over time, the clump at the center of the Solar System became more and more massive as the force of gravity attracted more and more matter. Eventually, the force of gravity became so intense and temperatures so high that nuclear fusion started in the core of this clump, releasing huge amounts of energy as heat and light—the Sun began to shine!

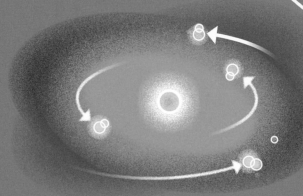

2. Growing clumps

When the Sun ignited, it blew away many of the lighter gases, leaving behind rocky clumps orbiting in a disc around the young glowing star.

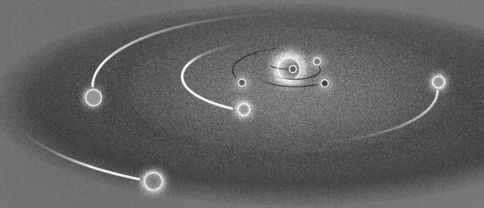

3. Protoplanets

The gravity from these clumps attracted more bits of rock and dust and they started to grow in size—a process called accretion. These growing clumps were known as protoplanets, the ancestors of today's planets.

4. The Solar System

The four planets closest to the Sun were rocky and quite small, while the four outermost planets were much larger and mainly formed from gas and ice.

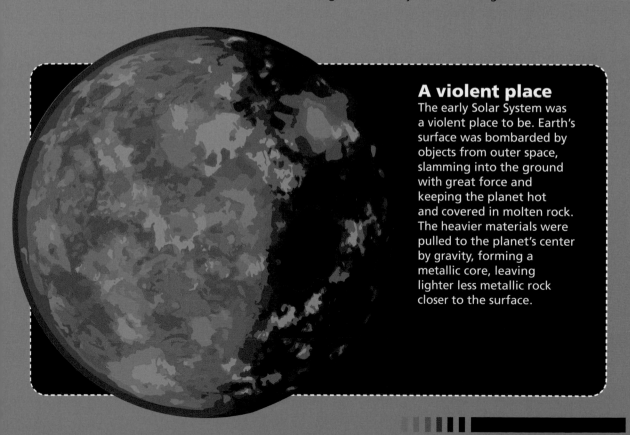

A violent place

The early Solar System was a violent place to be. Earth's surface was bombarded by objects from outer space, slamming into the ground with great force and keeping the planet hot and covered in molten rock. The heavier materials were pulled to the planet's center by gravity, forming a metallic core, leaving lighter less metallic rock closer to the surface.

Earth is the third planet from the Sun, after Mercury and Venus. This is the ideal position to make Earth a truly unique planet—the only place in the Universe that we know of where life exists!

Our planet's orbit

Earth travels around the Sun in an elliptical orbit that puts it about 93,000,000 miles (149,900,000 km) from the star on average.

At this distance it takes light about 8.5 minutes to travel from the Sun to Earth.

Earth is also moving at a velocity of 66,622 mph (107,218 kph), which means that it takes just over 365 days to complete one orbit around the Sun. This is why we have a leap year every four years.

Earth

Radius: **3,959 miles (6,371 km)**
Length of day: **23.9 hours**
Equatorial circumference: **24,873.6 miles (40,030.2 km)**
Surface area: 196,936,994 sq miles **510,064,472 km²**

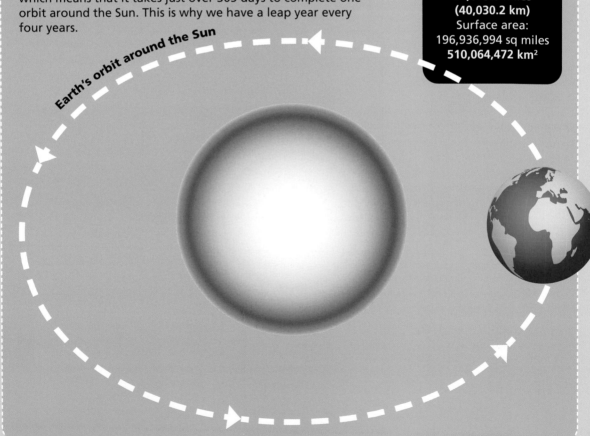

Earth's orbit around the Sun

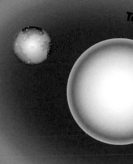

Too cold

Goldilocks zone

Too hot

The Goldilocks zone

Earth's orbit places it in a very special location in the Solar System—a region that astronomers call the habitable zone or Goldilocks zone. Just like the character tasting the bears' porridge in the fairytale, this zone is not too hot and not too cold, but just right for water to exist in its liquid form on the surface. Liquid water is essential for life to exist and it also helps to shape and mold the land.

Exoplanets

Astronomers have discovered distant planets that may be orbiting the Goldilocks zones of other stars. One of these is called Kepler-186f, and scientists believe that its surface may also have liquid water, so it could support alien life.

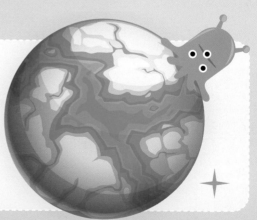

EARTH UNDER FIRE

After the violence of the early Solar System, the situation has calmed down and Earth is rarely hit by large objects. But every so often a big asteroid or comet has slammed into the surface, causing devastation.

Impact!

Larger objects do not completely burn up when they enter Earth's atmosphere and hit the surface with incredible force. The scorching temperatures create molten rock, which is flung away by the impact, forming a depression surrounded by a ring, called an impact crater.

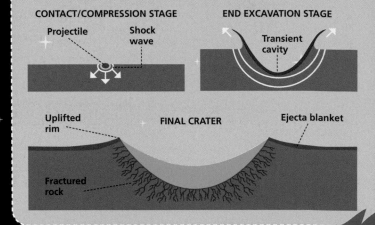

CONTACT/COMPRESSION STAGE

Projectile   Shock wave

END EXCAVATION STAGE

Transient cavity

Uplifted rim   FINAL CRATER   Ejecta blanket

Fractured rock

Extinction event

Perhaps the most famous impact occurred about 66 million years ago, when a lump of rock the size of a mountain crashed into Earth at what is now the Yucatan Peninsula, Mexico. The explosion threw up a cloud of gas and dust that blocked the Sun, killing plants and changing the climate for years. This violent event caused the extinction of the dinosaurs.

Meteors and shooting stars

Earth's atmosphere protects us from smaller objects, causing them to burn up harmlessly long before they can reach the surface. These meteors can leave long glowing streaks in the night sky, called shooting stars.

Hitting Earth

Every single day, Earth is hit by more than 100 tons of debris from outer space the size of dust and grains of sand. Once a year, an object the size of a car burns up in Earth's atmosphere, creating a fireball high in the air. Every 2,000 years, an object the size of a football field hits Earth, causing extensive damage. Every few million years, Earth is hit by an object that's so large it can cause a mass extinction event.

The largest meteorite ever discovered is the Hoba meteorite found in Namibia. It weighs

73 tons.

Near misses

Some objects pass close to Earth, to within 4.7 million miles (7.5 million m), and they are large enough to be classified as Potentially Hazardous Objects. Astronomers watch them carefully to see if they could hit Earth or pass harmlessly on their way.

THE MOON

Scientists believe that the Moon was formed when an object crashed into Earth about 4.5 billion years ago. The debris thrown up by this collision formed a ring around Earth. Over time, this debris joined to form the Moon.

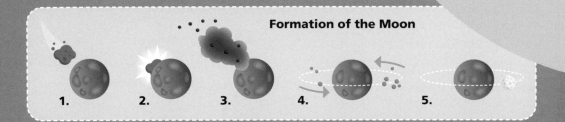

Formation of the Moon

1. 2. 3. 4. 5.

Controlling the tides

The gravitational force of the Moon pulls on the seas and oceans on Earth, causing them to bulge on either side of Earth. As Earth rotates beneath these bulges, so the seas rise and fall, causing the daily movement of the tides. The gravity of the Sun and Moon can act together to create especially high tides, called spring tides, or very low tides, called neap tides.

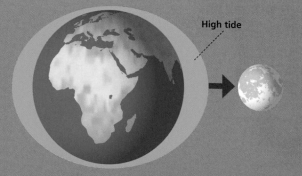

High tide

Phases of the Moon

The Moon spins around once in the same time it takes to orbit Earth. This means that we can only ever see one side of the Moon from our planet. As the Moon orbits Earth, the amount of its surface that is lit by the Sun changes, and the Moon appears to shrink and grow. These changes are called the phases of the Moon.

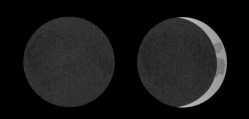

Moon

Average distance
from Earth:
238,855 miles (384,400 km)
Equatorial radius:
1,079.6 miles (1,737.5 km)
Equatorial circumference:
6,783.5 miles (10,917 km)
Surface area:
**14,647,439.75 sq miles
37,936,694.79 km²**

The Moon has its own atmosphere. It's called an
exosphere and is very thin and unbreathable.

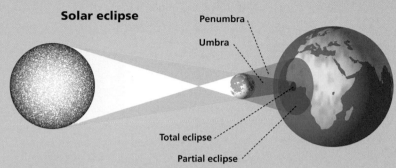

Solar eclipse

Penumbra

Umbra

Total eclipse

Partial eclipse

Highland area

Mare

Eclipse

When viewed from Earth, the Sun and Moon appear to
be exactly the same size. At certain times, the moon
passes in front of the Sun, blocking its light and causing
a solar eclipse. At other times, Earth passes between the
Sun and the Moon, blocking the Sun's light from reaching
the Moon and causing a lunar eclipse.

Seas and mountains

Seen from Earth, the surface of
the Moon is covered in dark
patches and brighter regions. The
darker areas are known as mare,
or seas, and were formed when
molten rock flowed out onto the
Moon's surface. The brighter
areas are highlands and
mountains that glow in the Sun's
light. Also visible are lots of
impact craters, formed when
rocks and objects hit the Moon
over millions of years.

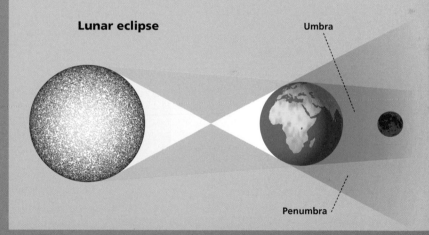

Lunar eclipse

Umbra

Penumbra

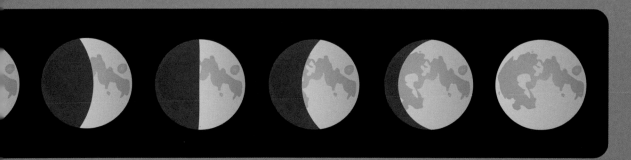

WHAT'S INSIDE EARTH?

Deep beneath Earth's surface, huge forces are at work, heating the metals and rocks beyond their melting point. At the same time, they are under so much pressure that most of them remain solid.

Nuclear center

Radioactive elements, such as uranium, deep within Earth's mantle release heat as they decay. This warms the inside of the planet and causes the forces that drive plate tectonics and shape the surface.

The core

Earth's core is made from metals, mainly iron and nickel. The inner core is a solid ball of metal, while the outer core is liquid.

The mantle

The mantle is rich in iron and is very hot, which makes it flow like thick tar. This swirling movement pulls on the crust above, causing it to crack apart into large plates of rock.

The crust

There are two types of crust—oceanic crust and continental crust. Oceanic crust forms the ocean floors. It is only about 5 miles (8 km) thick and made from basalt lava. The continental crust forms Earth's landmasses and can be up to 43 miles (70 km) thick and is made from many different types of rock.

The lower mantle is about
1,370 miles (2,200 km)
thick and temperatures there reach up to
5,430°F (3,000°C).

The crust is only about
**43 miles
(70 km)**
at its thickest.

The upper mantle is about **375 miles (600 km)** thick and temperatures there reach up to **1650°F (900°C).**

At the very center is the inner core made of nickel and iron, where temperatures can reach **9,750°F (5,400°C).**

Surrounding the inner core is the outer core, which is about **1,430 miles (2,300 km)** thick and made from nickel and iron fluids.

Crust   Mantle   Outer core   Inner core

GIANT MAGNET

The moving molten metal found in Earth's outer core churns about to produce a magnetic field around the planet. This magnetic field protects us from the Sun's harmful rays, helps us to find our way, and puts on an impressive light show.

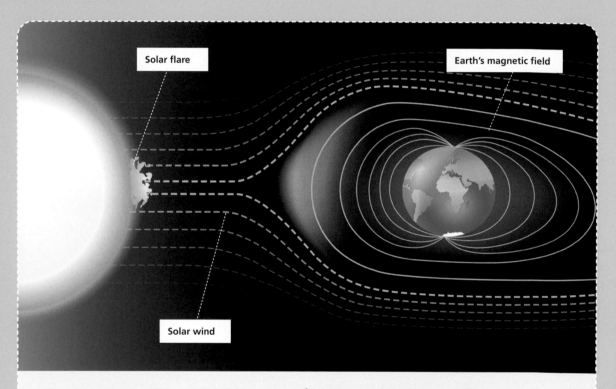

Solar flare

Earth's magnetic field

Solar wind

Magnetic Earth

As the metals in the outer core move and the planet spins, they produce an enormous magnetic field surrounding Earth. Like any other magnet, this field has two magnetic poles—a north and a south. The magnetic field stretches out into space, forming the magnetosphere.

The magnetosphere

The magnetosphere protects us from the Sun's charged particles, or solar wind, which would damage the ozone layer that protects us from harmful ultraviolet light. The solar wind squashes the side of the magnetosphere that faces the Sun.

Glowing lights

The magnetosphere deflects charged particles around Earth and down toward regions around the poles. Here, the particles interact with molecules in the air, creating the colorful glowing lights known as aurorae.

On the move

The magnetic poles are not located exactly at the actual poles and they move, sometimes by as much as 25 miles (40 km a year. Every 400,000 years or so, they swap over completely. Magnetic particles in newly-formed rocks line up in the opposite direction to older rocks, creating a striped pattern in their magnetic orientation.

Compasses

Magnetic compasses line up with Earth's magnetic field so that they point toward magnetic north. When the magnetic poles switch over, it's likely that compass needles will point in different directions for hundreds of years, before settling down to point south instead of north.

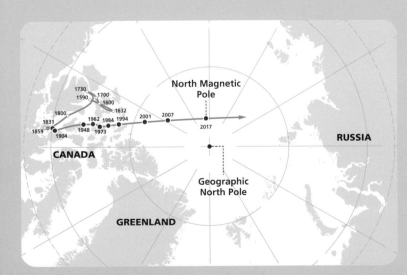

CHAPTER 2

CHANGING PLANET

A VIOLENT WORLD

Current in mantle

Core

Crust

It might not look like it, but Earth is changing all the time. Sometimes, these changes can take millions of years, but occasionally, they can be the result of very sudden and very violent events.

Volcanoes

Volcanoes occur where molten rock, called lava, spills out onto Earth's surface during an eruption.

Churning currents

Convection currents in the mantle push and pull on the crust above. Although the mantle is a solid, it behaves like a fluid over a very long time. One of the main causes of movement in Earth's crust is a process called slab pull. This is where colder and older tectonic plates sink beneath newer ones and into the mantle. This movement can produce some violent and dramatic events.

Earthquakes

The sudden shaking of the ground, or earthquake, is the result of a sudden release of energy when two large pieces of Earth's crust grind past each other.

Earth's crust isn't in one piece. Instead, it's broken up into several large pieces known as tectonic plates, which bump into each other, grind together, and pull apart.

North American Plate

Area: **29,305,000 sq miles (75,900,000 sq km)**
This plate forms most of North America and Iceland and is made up of both continental crust and oceanic crust.

A cracked surface

There are seven major tectonic plates that make up about 95 percent of Earth's surface, with the rest broken up into a number of smaller plates.

JUAN DE FUCA PLATE

CARIBBEAN PLATE

COCOS PLATE

NAZCA PLATE

PACIFIC PLATE

SCOTIA PLATE

South American Plate

Area: **16,834,000 sq miles (43,600,000 sq km)**
Including South America and much of the southern Atlantic, this plate is home to a lot of tectonic activity, leading to the formation of the tall Andes mountain chain and several volcanoes.

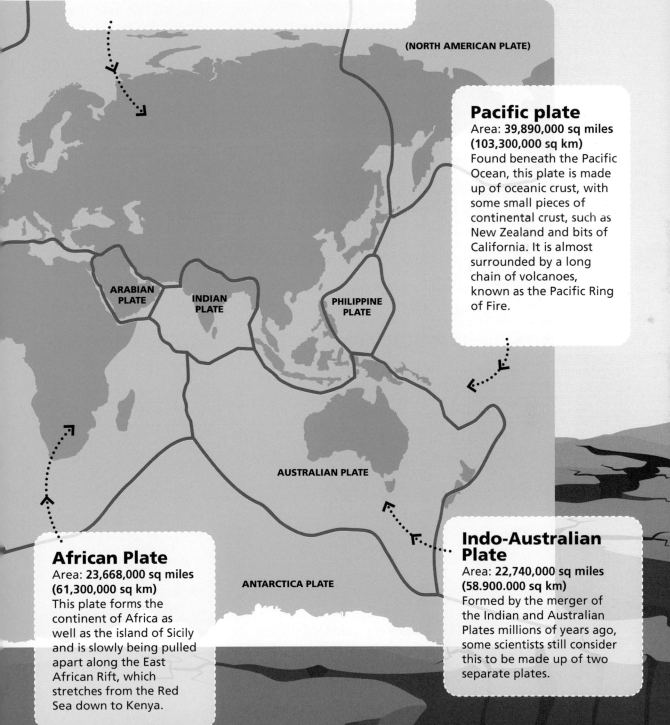

Eurasian Plate
Area: 26,178,000 sq miles (67,800,000 sq km)
Sitting beneath Europe and much of Asia, this plate is home to the Himalayas, formed by the collision between the Eurasian and Indian plates.

(NORTH AMERICAN PLATE)

Pacific plate
Area: 39,890,000 sq miles (103,300,000 sq km)
Found beneath the Pacific Ocean, this plate is made up of oceanic crust, with some small pieces of continental crust, such as New Zealand and bits of California. It is almost surrounded by a long chain of volcanoes, known as the Pacific Ring of Fire.

ARABIAN PLATE

INDIAN PLATE

PHILIPPINE PLATE

AUSTRALIAN PLATE

African Plate
Area: 23,668,000 sq miles (61,300,000 sq km)
This plate forms the continent of Africa as well as the island of Sicily and is slowly being pulled apart along the East African Rift, which stretches from the Red Sea down to Kenya.

ANTARCTICA PLATE

Indo-Australian Plate
Area: 22,740,000 sq miles (58.900.000 sq km)
Formed by the merger of the Indian and Australian Plates millions of years ago, some scientists still consider this to be made up of two separate plates.

As Earth's tectonic plates move about, they drag the landmasses along with them, changing the map of Earth over hundreds of millions of years.

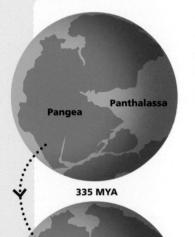

Pangea **Panthalassa**

335 MYA

Laurasia

Gondwanaland

200 MYA

200-50 MYA

Super continent

About 335 million years ago (MYA), all of Earth's landmasses were joined together to form a huge supercontinent called Pangea. This was surrounded by a huge ocean known as Panthalassa.

Splitting up

Some 200 million years ago, Pangea was torn apart to form two large continents, with Laurasia in the north and Gondwanaland in the south.

Forming the continents

Over the next 150 million years, the two larger continents broke apart into smaller ones. Laurasia divided into North America and Eurasia, with the Atlantic Ocean forming in between them. Gondwanaland split up into South America, Antarctica, Africa, India, and Australia.

North America
Area:
**9,540,198 sq miles
(24,709,000)**
Percentage of land area:
16.5%

South America
Area:
**6,888,060 sq miles
(17,840,000 sq km)**
Percentage of land area:
12.0%

The world today

Today's world map has six main landmasses. These are North America, South America, Africa, Eurasia (Europe and Asia), Australia, and Antarctica.

Europe
Area:
**3,930,520 sq miles
(10,180,000 sq km)**
Percentage of land area:
6.8%

Asia
Area:
**17,212,050 sq miles
(44,579,000 sq km)**
Percentage of land area:
29.5%

Africa
Area:
**11,725,923 sq miles
(30,370,000)**
Percentage of land area:
20.4%

Australia
Area:
**3,320,000 sq miles
(8,600,000 sq km)**
Percentage of land area:
5.8%

Antarctica
Area:
**5,405,430 sq miles
(14,000,000 sq km)**
Percentage of land area:
9.0%

The places where two or more tectonic plates meet are called plate boundaries. Here, huge forces tear the plates apart, slam them into each other, or grind them together with powerful and destructive effects.

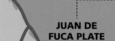

JUAN DE FUCA PLATE

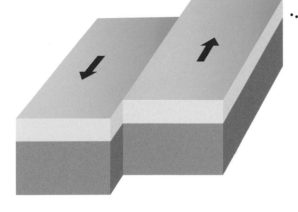

Transform boundaries

Transform boundaries occur where two or more plates scrape past each other. Friction between the two plates can slow down movement, which is then released suddenly triggering an earthquake. One example of a transform boundary is the San Andreas Fault in California, USA.

Every year the Atlantic Basin is growing at a rate of between **½ to 4 inches (1–10 cm).**

Divergent boundaries

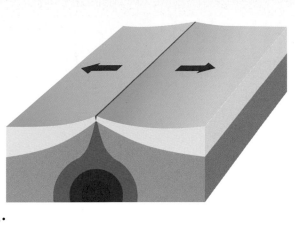

Where two tectonic plates pull apart is called a divergent boundary. As the two plates move away, magma wells up between them forming volcanoes and a long ridge where the liquid rock cools. The Mid-Atlantic ridge is an underwater chain of mountains that runs about 9,940 miles (16,000 km) from the Arctic Ocean right down to the Southern Ocean, forming the longest mountain range on Earth.

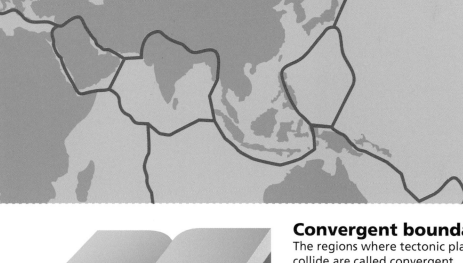

Convergent boundaries

The regions where tectonic plates collide are called convergent boundaries. Where oceanic crust collides with continental crust, then the more-dense oceanic crust is pushed down into Earth's mantle. Friction melts the rock and can cause earthquakes, while plumes of molten magma can rise to the surface, bursting through in volcanic eruptions and creating a chain of volcanic mountains. This can be seen where the Nazca Plate collides with the South America plate, creating the Andes mountain chain in South America.

When two pieces of continental crust collide, they both pile up, creating fold mountains.

EARTHQUAKES

Friction can stop tectonic plates moving against each other. Eventually, the force builds up so much that it is suddenly released in an earthquake.

Causing quakes

Most earthquakes occur close to plate boundaries where the plates are rubbing against each other, but they can occur near the middle of plates. As the two plates slide against each other, friction causes them to stop moving and stress to build up in the rocks on either side of the boundary. Eventually, the stress in the rocks is so great that the plates slip suddenly, releasing huge amounts of energy that travel out in seismic waves, like ripples on a pond.

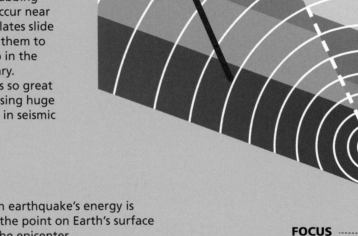

EPICENTER

FOCUS

The center

The point in Earth's crust where an earthquake's energy is released is called the focus, while the point on Earth's surface directly above the focus is called the epicenter.

Measuring earthquakes

The strength of an earthquake is called its magnitude and it is measured using the Richter scale, from 1 to 10. Each increase in number represents a tenfold increase in the power of an earthquake, so an earthquake with a magnitude of 8.0 is ten times more powerful than one with a magnitude of 7.

Micro	Minor		Light	Moderate
1.0-1.9	2.0-2.9	3.0-3.9	4.0-4.9	5.0-5.9

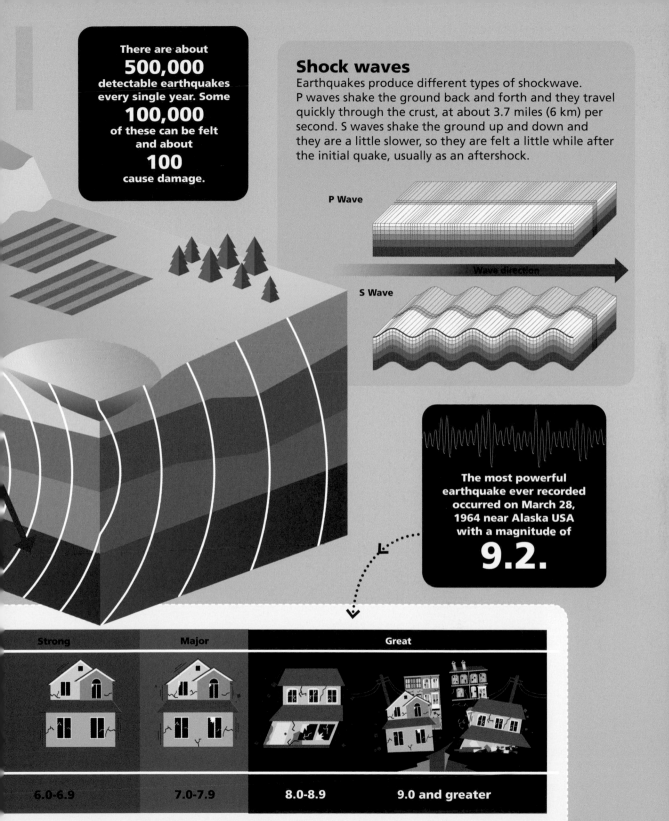

There are about **500,000** detectable earthquakes every single year. Some **100,000** of these can be felt and about **100** cause damage.

Shock waves

Earthquakes produce different types of shockwave. P waves shake the ground back and forth and they travel quickly through the crust, at about 3.7 miles (6 km) per second. S waves shake the ground up and down and they are a little slower, so they are felt a little while after the initial quake, usually as an aftershock.

P Wave

Wave direction

S Wave

The most powerful earthquake ever recorded occurred on March 28, 1964 near Alaska USA with a magnitude of **9.2.**

Strong	Major	Great	
6.0-6.9	7.0-7.9	8.0-8.9	9.0 and greater

TSUNAMIS

When an earthquake occurs on the sea floor it can trigger a huge wave that travels across the ocean, rearing up when it reaches land to crash onto the shore, causing huge amounts of damage.

Out at sea

The sudden movement of tectonic plates on the sea bed triggers an earthquake and displaces a huge amount of water above it. This displacement travels out from the site of the earthquake. Out at sea in deep water, tsunamis will travel very quickly at speeds of up to 500 miles (800 km) per hour, but they will only have a height, or amplitude, of about 20 to 24 inches (50 to 60 cm).

The word **"tsunami"** comes from the Japanese meaning **"harbor wave."**

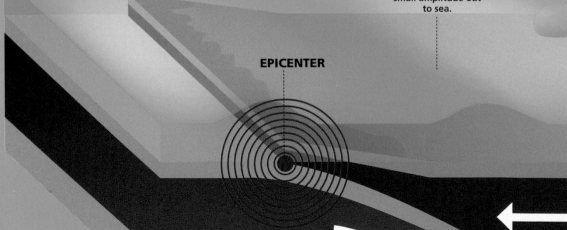

A tsunami has a small amplitude out to sea.

EPICENTER

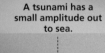

Powerful tsunamis

Tsunamis can travel for thousands of miles from their source, causing damage on the other side of the world.

An earthquake in 1958 caused a tsunami that roared into Lituya Bay, Alaska, USA, and caused damage up to an elevation (height) of 1,719 feet (524 m), snapping trees and clearing about 1.5 square miles (4 sq km) of woodland.

The explosive eruption of the Krakatoa volcano in August 1883 created a wave that was 115 feet (35 m) high.

An earthquake off the Indonesian island of Sumatra in 2004 created a powerful tsunami that raced across the Indian Ocean, hitting India and Sri Lanka with waves up to 29 feet (9 m) high in just two hours and reaching the east coast of Africa more than 3,000 kilometres away. In total, more than 200,000 were killed from Thailand to Somalia.

In 1960, a powerful earthquake off the coast of Chile caused a tsunami that raced across the Pacific causing damage in Hawaii 15 hours after the earthquake and hitting Japan 22 hours after the initial shock.

Wave grows in size as it nears the shore.

Close to shore

As a tsunami approaches the shore, friction with the seafloor slows the wave down. As the wave slows, its height increases dramatically. As the first trough of the wave reaches the shore, the sea waters pull back, revealing the seafloor. Then the powerful wave crashes on the shore, carrying boats far inland, uprooting trees and knocking down buildings. The water then pulls back to the sea, causing even more damage.

BUILDING MOUNTAINS

The continuous movement of Earth's tectonic plates throws up rocks to form towering mountain peaks that can be found on their own or in long chains that stretch for many hundreds of miles.

Hawaii

The islands of Hawaii are formed by tall volcanic peaks that stick out above the Pacific Ocean. These volcanoes formed in hot spots in the Pacific plate.

SOUTH AMERICA

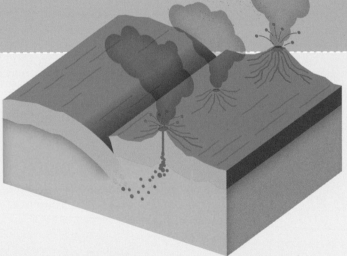

Volcanic mountains

Deep beneath the surface, molten magma pushes upward, forcing the rocks above it to rise to form mountains. In some places, the liquid rock can erupt onto the surface to form volcanic peaks. Many of these mountains form close to convergent plate boundaries, but some volcanoes form in the middle of tectonic plates, where the crust is thin and magma can well up to the surface. These places are called hot spots.

Himalayas

The Himalayas formed when the Indian plate collided with the Eurasian plate pushing up what had been sea floor between the two landmasses to form the highest mountain range on the planet. As the Indian plate continues to push north, the Himalayas are growing at a rate of about 1 inch (2.5 cm) every year.

ASIA

AFRICA

INDIA

Fold mountains

When two plates of continental crust crash into each other, they are folded together and pushed upward to form fold mountains.

East African Rift Valley

Eastern Africa is being torn apart as two plates, the African and Somali, move away from each other. This has created two sets of mountains including the Mitumba Mountains and the Rwenzori Range in the west and the snowy peaks of Mount Kenya and Kilimanjaro in the east.

Block mountains

These mountains are formed when a block of land is pushed up by tectonic movement, or when two plates move apart, causing the land between them to drop down and leaving two mountain chains on either side.

VOLCANIC ERUPTIONS

When red-hot magma pushes up from Earth's mantle it can break through the crust, forming a volcanic eruption and pouring lava, gas, ash, and rocks onto the surrounding countryside.

Types of volcano

The materials thrown out by an eruption decide what type of volcano is involved:

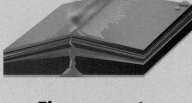

Layers of ash

Lava flow

Shield Volcano

If the lava is runny with a low viscosity then it will flow quite far before cooling and solidifying. This will form a volcano with wide, shallow sides, called a shield volcano. Mauna Kea and Mauna Loa in Hawaii are both shield volcanoes.

Fissure vent Volcano

Lava may erupt through a long crack in the surface to form a fissure vent.

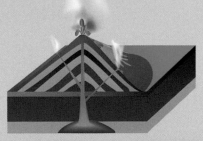

Stratovolcano

If the lava is very thick, then it won't flow very far before cooling and solidifying. This will form a volcano with steep sides, called a stratovolcano, or composite volcano, because it will contain layers of both rock and ash.

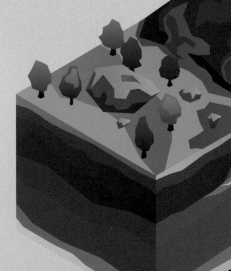

Inside a volcano

Hot magma rises to the surface because it is less dense than the surrounding rock, carrying trapped gases with it and causing the land above to bulge. When the pressure becomes too great, the molten rock, gas, dust, and rocks burst through a vent.

Volcanic dangers

As well as red-hot liquid lava, volcanoes release and cause other dangers:

- Pyroclastic flows are clouds of super-hot rock, gas, and dust that roll down the sides of a volcano at speeds of up to 435 miles (700 km) per hour, incinerating everything in their way.

- The power of an eruption can dislodge huge flows of mud, called lahars, which sweep down the volcano burying entire towns and villages.

- Volcanic bombs are large pieces of rock that are thrown out by the volcano and slam into the surrounding countryside.

- Volcanic ash can contain small rocks and bits of volcanic glass. In severe eruptions, the ash can be so thick that it makes breathing dangerous and it can fall on buildings causing them to collapse under the added weight. Volcanic ash can also be dangerous for planes flying overhead as it can clog jet engines, causing them to fail.

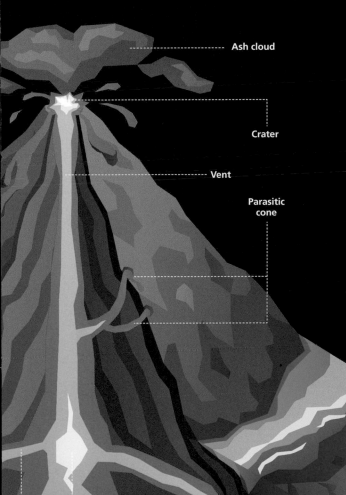

Ash cloud

Crater

Vent

Parasitic cone

Sill

Laccolith

Magma chamber

WHERE ARE VOLCANOES?

Most of the world's volcanoes are found on or near plate boundaries. At convergent boundaries, the action of one plate being pushed into the mantle causes magma to rise to the surface where it bursts through to form volcanoes. At divergent boundaries, magma wells up to fill the gap left when the tectonic plates pull apart.

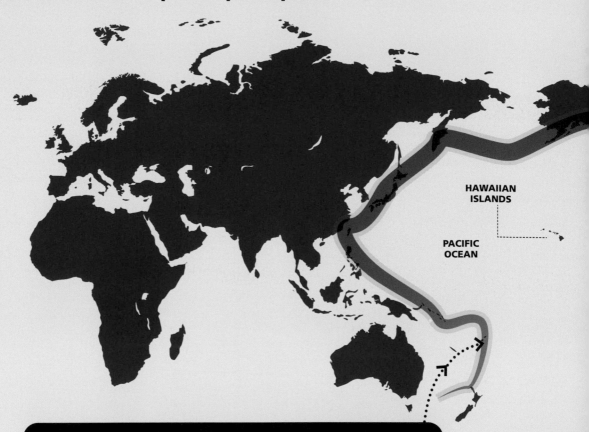

HAWAIIAN ISLANDS

PACIFIC OCEAN

Pacific Ring of Fire

Surrounding much of the Pacific Ocean is a region that contains about 75 percent of the world's active volcanoes. This horseshoe-shaped area is known as the Pacific Ring of Fire and it stretches for about 25,000 miles (40,000 km) from New Zealand up through Asia, Japan, across the Bering Straits, down North America, and south to the tip of South America.

Hotspots

Some volcanoes are found far from plate boundaries in areas known as hotspots. As the tectonic plate moves over the hotspot, it creates a line or chain of volcanoes, such as the Hawaiian islands in the Pacific.

If they were measured from their bases, Mauna Kea, Hawaii, is actually taller than Mount Everest.

Mount Everest

Mauna Kea

Sea level

Surtsey

In November 1963, an undersea volcano off the coast of Iceland erupted. Within a few days it had grown a cone that broke the surface of the water, creating a brand new island, which became known as Surtsey. Today, the island reaches an elevation of more than 492 feet (150 m) and scientists predict it will stay above the waves for another 100 years before it is eroded by the sea.

Parícutin

The eruption of Parícutin in 1943 caught everyone by surprise. The volcano suddenly appeared in the middle of a farmer's cornfield and in the nine years it was active, it grew to a height of 1,391 feet (424 m) and had damaged an area of more than 88.8 square miles (230 km sq).

Supervolcanoes

In some places, magma wells up from the mantle but is unable to force its way to the surface. It continues to build up, forming a huge chamber of magma, which, when the pressure is great enough will explode onto the surface as an enormous supervolcano. Fortunately, these eruptions are very rare and scientists believe that there have been just 42 in the last 36 million years.

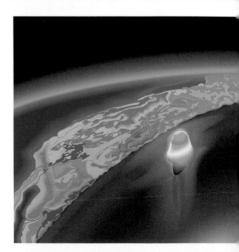

An enormous magma chamber sits below Yellowstone National Park, Wyoming, USA.

HOT SPRINGS AND GEYSERS

Where surface water soaks down, or percolates, through rocks and comes into contact with hot volcanic rocks, the results can sometimes be spectacular.

Geysers

If a hot spring has a restriction in the tubes carrying the water back to the surface, then the water can build up, increasing the pressure. When the pressure gets high enough, the super-hot water shoots to the surface under high pressure, producing a tall fountain known as a geyser.

Hot springs

Rain water percolates down through the rock and is warmed by volcanic rocks underground. The water can then rise to the surface without being trapped to form pools of hot water, known as hot springs. These springs can be surrounded by brightly colored minerals deposited by the heated water.

Fumaroles

Fumaroles are produced if the water boils away before reaching the surface. As the steam rushes out through a hole in the ground, it produces a whistling or hissing sound.

Mudpots

Water trapped in a depression on the surface is heated by steam from underground. Microbes feed on hydrogen sulfide gas that is present producing sulfuric acid which melts any clay in the soil, creating a bubbling bowl of mud.

Steamboat Geyser in Yellowstone National Park, Wyoming, USA, is the largest geyser in the world, and can shoot steam and water up to a height of 330 feet (100 m).

Travertine terraces

If a hot spring rises up through limestone, then the water dissolves the calcium carbonate as it climbs, before depositing it at the surface to form brightly colored terraces with pools of water.

Using this energy

Some countries have used the power from hydrothermal springs and vents to produce electricity. More than a quarter of Iceland's electricity is produced by geothermal power stations.

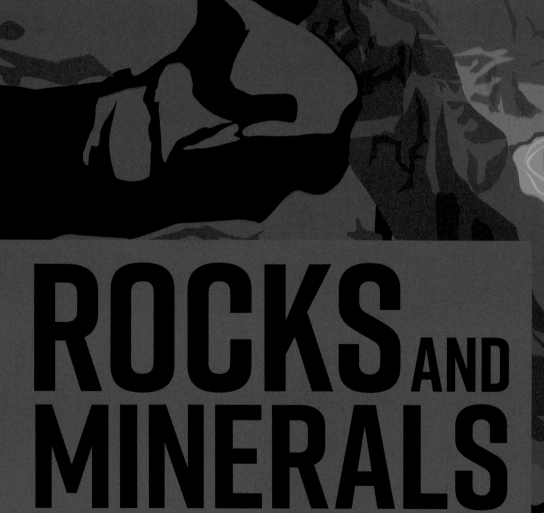

CHAPTER 3

ROCKS AND MINERALS

HARD ROCK

We are surrounded by rocks and minerals as they form the part of the outer crust of Earth. Minerals are chemical structures that form rocks.

Elements

There are about 90 elements that occur naturally on Earth. Many of these elements react with each other to form compounds, for example oxygen and hydrogen will join together to form water. Others, such as gold, do not react well with other elements and they are usually found in their pure form.

Minerals

Minerals are solid compounds that usually have a crystal-like structure, and these combine together to form the rocks that make up Earth. For example, the rock granite contains the minerals quartz, feldspar, and mica.

Metals

Metals are shiny elements that are very good at conducting electricity and heat. Many of them will also react with other elements creating a type of mineral called a metal ore. Iron, for example, will react with oxygen to form iron oxide, otherwise known as rust.

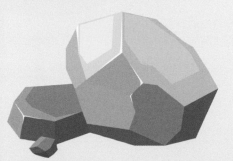

Crystals

Crystals are formed when minerals take on a regular geometric shape and they are usually formed when molten rock or dissolved minerals solidify.

THE ROCK CYCLE

Earth's rocks may look like they've been around forever, but they are always changing as the processes of plate tectonics and the actions of the world around them transform them from one type of rock to another in a constant cycle.

Rock types

There are three main types of rock:

Igneous rock—formed from cooling liquid lava.
Metamorphic rock—rocks with a structure that has been changed by intense heat and/or pressure
Sedimentary rock—formed from tiny particles that have been squeezed together.

Magma

Eruptions and intrusions

Deep underground, high temperatures melt rock to form magma. This magma can rise toward the surface and cool to form solid underground lumps of igneous rock, or it can erupt onto the surface as lava before cooling into solid rock.

Melting

Igneous rock

Weathering and erosion

The actions of the wind, rain, flowing water, hot and cold temperatures, and even growing plants can break up rocks into tiny pieces that are then carried away. These processes are called weathering and erosion and they can expose bits of rock that were buried.

Melting

If the temperatures are high enough, then any rocks are melted to form magma and the cycle starts over again.

Pressure and heat

Underground, rocks are subjected to very high pressures and temperatures. This can change the chemical structure of rocks to form entirely new metamorphic rocks.

Pushing up and down

The actions of plate tectonics move large pieces of rock, dragging some deep below the surface, a process called subduction, or pushing them back up in a process called upheaval.

Metamorphic rock

Melting

Temperature and pressure

Weathering and erosion

Weathering and erosion

Sedimentation and compaction

Tiny pieces of rock that are carried by streams and rivers are known as sediment. Eventually, these are dropped at the bottom of lakes and seas in a process called sedimentation. As more layers are dropped, the sediment is squeezed, or compacted, to form solid sedimentary rock.

Sedimentary rock

IGNEOUS ROCKS

Deep inside Earth, high temperatures melt rocks to form magma. When it cools, magma solidifies to form igneous rocks.

Magma and lava

In Earth's mantle, the pressures are so great that any rock there is kept solid, even though the temperatures are very high. However, if the pressure is reduced or the melting point of the rock lowered by adding water, then the rock can melt and rise up toward the crust as magma. If it breaks through the crust onto the surface, it is then called lava.

Rocky crystals

Igneous rocks are made up of small crystals that interlock with each other to form hard, solid stone. The size of these crystals depends on where the rock solidifies and how quickly this happens. Igneous rocks that cool quickly have very small crystals, while those that cool slowly have large crystals.

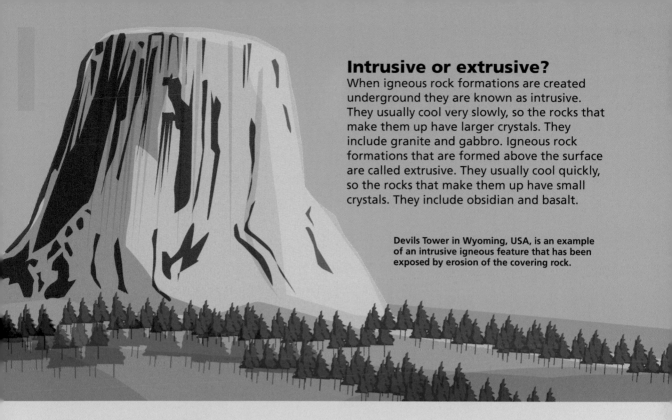

Intrusive or extrusive?

When igneous rock formations are created underground they are known as intrusive. They usually cool very slowly, so the rocks that make them up have larger crystals. They include granite and gabbro. Igneous rock formations that are formed above the surface are called extrusive. They usually cool quickly, so the rocks that make them up have small crystals. They include obsidian and basalt.

Devils Tower in Wyoming, USA, is an example of an intrusive igneous feature that has been exposed by erosion of the covering rock.

Igneous formations

Igneous rocks can form many different-shaped rock formations as they push up through the layers of Earth's crust.

Volcanic plugs form when magma inside a volcano's vent cools and hardens.

Smaller domes, called laccoliths, form between layers of rock.

Thin sills squeeze between layers of rock.

Dykes are formed by molten rock pushing up between vertical cracks in the rocks.

Enormous domes called batholiths can measure hundreds of miles across.

SEDIMENTARY ROCKS

Sedimentary rocks are formed from the eroded particles of other rocks or the remains of living things that are deposited in layers and squeezed and cemented together until they form hard stone.

From transport to cementation

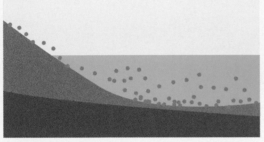

1. Small pieces of rock are broken up and transported away by wind or water.

2. Eventually, these small pieces of rock are deposited on the bed of a river, lake, or the sea.

3. Layers of this sediment build up over millions of years. The weight of the upper layers of sediment squeezes the lower layers; a process called compaction.

4. Compaction squeezes water out from between the pieces of rock, leaving crystals to form. These crystals hold the pieces of rock together. This is called cementation.

Layers and layers

As sedimentary rock is laid down over time, it can form clear layers and stripes in the rocks. Geologists can then use these stripes to date the rocks and see how any movement of the land has bent or broken these layers over time.

Younger rocks

Older rocks

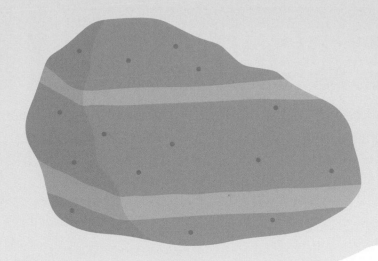

Sandstone

Sandstone is formed from tiny grains of sand that have been cemented together.

Limestone and chalk

Some types of limestone are made from deposits of calcite that have formed from lime dissolved in seawater. Others are made up of the skeletons and shells of tiny sea creatures that have been deposited on the sea floor over millions of years.

Conglomerate

Conglomerates are made up of large pebbles of different sizes that have been cemented together. They are also known as puddingstones because the large stones look like the pieces of fruit in a pudding.

Coal

The remains of plants that become waterlogged may not decay. Instead, they can build up over the years to form a layer of peat. If this peat is then buried and compressed for millions of years it will slowly turn into coal.

Fossils are the remains or traces of living things that have been trapped in sedimentary rock and turned into stone. This process can take thousands or even millions of years.

Becoming a fossil

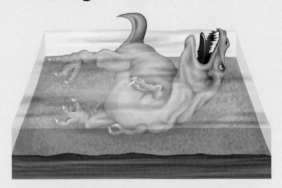

1. The living thing dies and its soft body parts are eaten by scavengers or start to rot away.

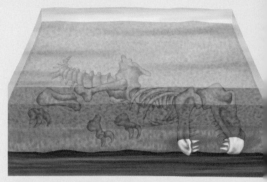

2. The remains are buried by sediments, such as mud or sand.

4. Water seeps into the remains and deposits minerals, turning the remains into stone.

5. The surrounding rock is either pushed up or eroded away to expose the fossil.

The fossilized remains of sea creatures have been found close to the summit of Mount Everest, the highest place on Earth.

Fossil poop

Coprolites are the fossilized remains of animal dung. This preserved poop can tell scientists what animal they came from and a lot about what the animal ate at the time, whether that was the remains of another animal or leaves and seeds from plants.

Trace fossils

Living things don't just leave behind their body parts as evidence of their existence. They can also leave impressions as they go about their lives, such as the pattern of their skin or feathers or footprints in the muddy ground. These are then turned to stone as trace fossils and they can tell a lot about how a creature lived.

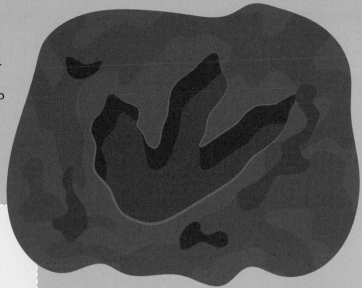

3. As more layers of sediment build up on top, the layers below are turned into sedimentary rock.

Fossils are usually only found in sedimentary rock as they do not survive the intense heat and pressure that forms igneous and metamorphic rocks.

Fine details

Some fossils have preserved animals in incredible detail. These include the delicate wings on prehistoric insects and the feathers on some dinosaur bodies. Scientists have even found the remains of cells in fossil feathers that may provide clues about the colors of feathered dinosaurs.

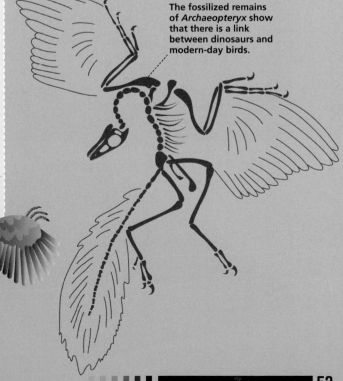

The fossilized remains of *Archaeopteryx* show that there is a link between dinosaurs and modern-day birds.

METAMORPHIC ROCKS

As Earth's tectonic plates move about, large pieces of rock are pushed down into Earth's crust where high pressures and intense temperatures can turn them into a completely different type of rock.

Heated and squeezed

Igneous, sedimentary, and metamorphic rocks are changed by intense heat, high pressures, and the presence of a mineral-rich fluid (or a combination of these). The temperatures are high, up to 930°F (500°C), but they aren't high enough to actually melt the rock. Instead, they turn it into metamorphic rock. For example, chalk and limestone are converted into marble, while layers of soft shale, a sedimentary rock, are converted into slate.

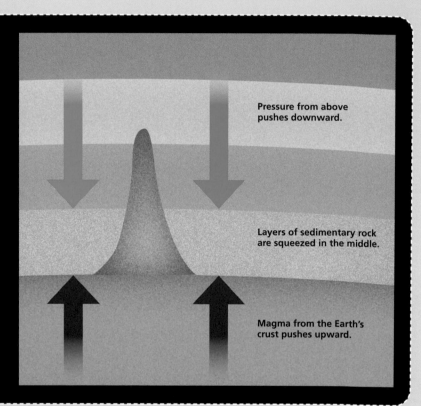

Pressure from above pushes downward.

Layers of sedimentary rock are squeezed in the middle.

Magma from the Earth's crust pushes upward.

Slate

When layers of shale are squeezed by the tectonic forces that form mountain ranges, the minerals inside the shale break down and settle into thin layers of slate. Slate is harder than shale, but it also splits easily to form thin sheets, making it an ideal material for roof tiles.

Marble

When chalk and limestone are compressed and heated they recrystallize to form marble. Marble comes in a wide range of colors, from deep red with wavy lines running through it to pure white. The stone is hard, but easy to chisel and carve, which is why it is an ideal material for statues. However, marble can be attacked chemically by acids, which is why many old buildings and statues have been damaged over the years by acid rain caused by pollution.

Marble has been used by sculptors for thousands of years to carve statues and busts.

Gneiss

Gneiss is formed from granite and is made up of rough crystals that interlock with each other. The crystals form pale and dark layers so that the rock has a striped appearance.

When rocks are brought to the surface, they come under attack from the weather, water, and even plants. These break rocks down into smaller pieces that are then carried away and dumped elsewhere.

Weathering

The process of breaking rocks up into smaller pieces is known as weathering.

Hot and cold

In some parts of the world, day and night-time temperatures can vary wildly, causing rocks to expand as they heat up in the day, and contract as they cool at night. This can cause the outer layers of rocks to crack and break away.

Acid

Acid dissolved in rainwater can eat away at some rocks, such as limestone. This opens up cracks or fissures and can form underground caves.

Plants and microbes

Some rocks are attacked by tiny microbes that feed on the minerals inside them. Plant roots can push through rocks, breaking them apart as they grow down in search of water.

Freezing water

Water can seep into the cracks in rocks and, if the temperature drops enough, it will freeze into ice. As it freezes, the water expands and pushes against the rock, cracking it apart and breaking it up into smaller pieces.

Erosion

Erosion is the process of breaking up and removing small pieces of rock and minerals.

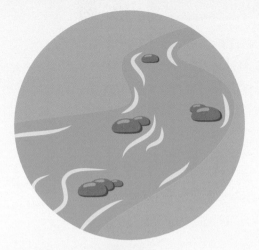

Water

The moving water of a stream or river can carry away small pieces of rock. If the current is strong enough, then larger stones and boulders are pushed along as well. The small pieces of rock also bump, scratch and scour larger rocks and stones along the river bed, wearing them smooth.

Waves

The powerful crashing of waves along the seashore erodes rock and creates many coastal features, including caves, arches, and stacks.

Glaciers

High in mountain ranges, icy glaciers flow slowly along valleys. As they move along, they tear away pieces of rock and scrape them along the ground, breaking away more rock and shaping the land.

Wind

Strong winds can pick up tiny pieces of rocks and minerals and hurl them against larger rock structures, sand-blasting and eroding them.

SOIL

Many parts of the world are covered in a layer of broken rock and mineral pieces mixed with the decaying remains of plants, animals, and other organisms, as well as water and gases. This layer is known as soil.

Types of soil

There are three main types of soil: clay, silt, and sand.

Sandy soils have particles that measure 0.05–2 mm.

Silt soils have particles that measure 0.002–0.05 mm.

Clay soils have particles that measure less than 0.002 mm.

A clay mineral called smectite swells and shrinks so much when it absorbs and loses water that it can knock over buildings.

Soil layers

Soils are usually divided up into layers, called horizons. The top layers are rich in decaying organic matter. Below these are layers of minerals and rocks, with the solid bedrock at the base.

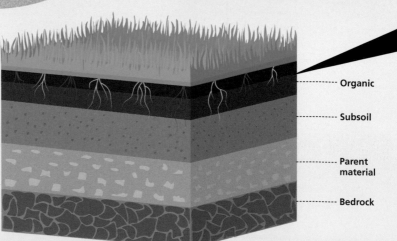

Organic

Subsoil

Parent material

Bedrock

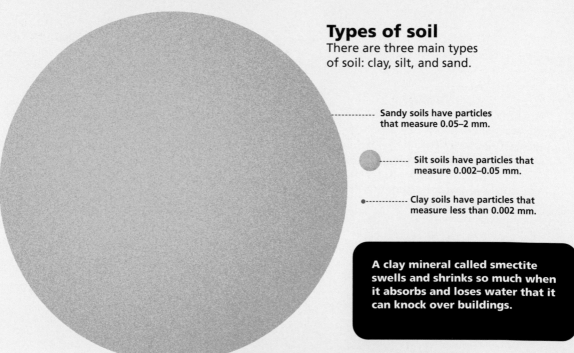

Teeming with life

The bodies of living things, such as fallen trees and dead animals, are broken down by bacteria, fungi and other living things. This creates a dark crumbly material called humus, which is rich in nutrients. Tiny soil microbes feed off these nutrients and plants use them to grow. These nutrients, microbes, and plants are, in turn, food for other animals.

Rich and fertile

Most of the elements and water essential for plants to grow can be found in soils. Those soils that are high in nutrients are good for growing crops. Sandy soils tend to lose water easily, while clay soils make it difficult for plants to draw water up through their roots. Silt soils can hold onto their water, but still make it easy for plants to get the water they need to thrive.

A single teaspoon of soil can contain more than a billion bacteria.

Soil erosion

The loss of the soil layer can be devastating to an area and stop all plants from growing. Many human activities, such as poor farming and pollution, can damage the soil and erode it. A build-up of salts, a process called salinization, can make it impossible for plants to survive.

CHAPTER 4

BLUE PLANET

WATER WORLD

Earth has so much water that, when seen from space, our planet looks like a blue ball with some small patches of land and ice. Earth is the only place we know of in the Universe where water exists in all three states—solid ice, liquid water, and gassy vapor.

Liquid water

Earth's blue appearance is down to the huge seas and oceans that cover most of its surface. Liquid water is also found flowing along streams and rivers and collecting in lakes. It also flows beneath the surface in underground rivers and seeping through rocks and soil.

Solid water

In the colder parts of the world, close to the poles and high up mountains, water is frozen solid to form huge ice sheets and glaciers. So much water is held in these sheets of ice that if the Greenland ice sheet were to melt, its waters could raise sea levels around the planet by about 23 feet (7 m).

Gassy water

Water vapor forms about 2–3 percent of Earth's atmosphere. It is usually invisible, but it can condense to form tiny droplets that gather to form clouds. If these droplets become heavy enough, they will fall to the ground as rain.

WHERE IS THE WATER?

Most of Earth's surface is covered by water, but a lot of this is too salty for us to drink or is locked up deep underground or frozen solid in glaciers, leaving only a small proportion that we can use.

If you took all of the water that is on, above and under Earth it would measure about 332.5 million cubic miles (1.386 billion cubic kilometres) and make a ball that measures about

860 miles
(1,385 kilometres)
in diameter.

Where is Earth's water?
The vast majority of Earth's water is held in the seas and oceans, with just a tiny amount found elsewhere, such as rivers, lakes, and groundwater.

Seas and oceans
96.54%

Water from space
Scientists believe that water was brought to Earth on water-rich meteorites and comets that collided with the young planet during the early years of its formation.

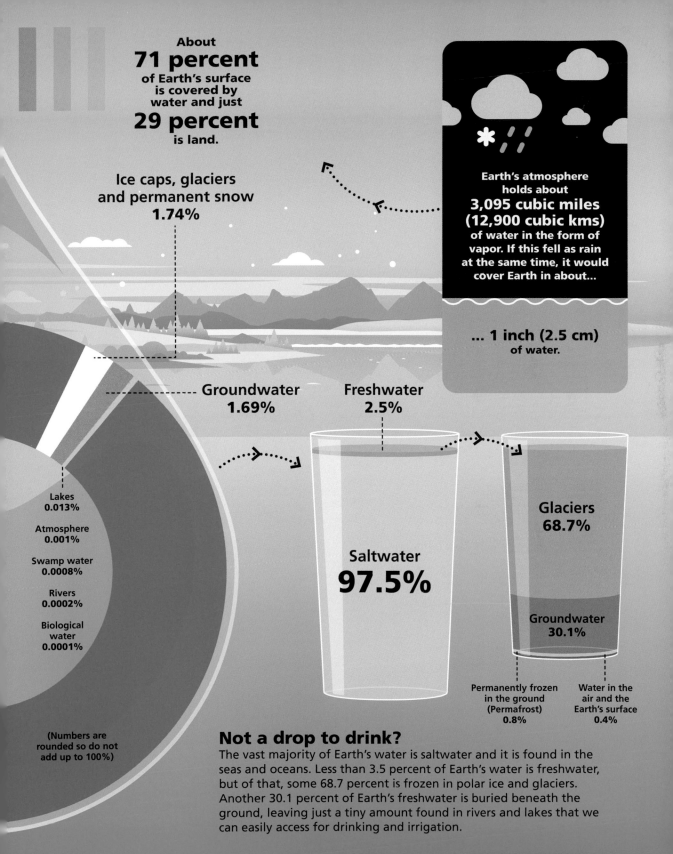

About
71 percent
of Earth's surface
is covered by
water and just
29 percent
is land.

Earth's atmosphere
holds about
**3,095 cubic miles
(12,900 cubic kms)**
of water in the form of
vapor. If this fell as rain
at the same time, it would
cover Earth in about...

... 1 inch (2.5 cm)
of water.

Ice caps, glaciers
and permanent snow
1.74%

Groundwater
1.69%

Freshwater
2.5%

Lakes
0.013%

Atmosphere
0.001%

Swamp water
0.0008%

Rivers
0.0002%

Biological
water
0.0001%

Saltwater
97.5%

Glaciers
68.7%

Groundwater
30.1%

Permanently frozen
in the ground
(Permafrost)
0.8%

Water in the
air and the
Earth's surface
0.4%

(Numbers are
rounded so do not
add up to 100%)

Not a drop to drink?

The vast majority of Earth's water is saltwater and it is found in the
seas and oceans. Less than 3.5 percent of Earth's water is freshwater,
but of that, some 68.7 percent is frozen in polar ice and glaciers.
Another 30.1 percent of Earth's freshwater is buried beneath the
ground, leaving just a tiny amount found in rivers and lakes that we
can easily access for drinking and irrigation.

THE WATER CYCLE

All the water on Earth is going through a continuous cycle, changing from one state to another as it moves around the planet.

Solid, liquid, gas

Water on Earth can be found in all three states of matter: as solid ice in glaciers and ice caps, liquid water in seas and rivers, and as gassy water vapor in the atmosphere.

Precipitation
Water falls to the ground as precipitation —rain, sleet, or snow.

Runoff
Water moves downhill in a process called runoff, collecting into streams and rivers that flow into lakes and seas.

Percolation
Water sinks, or percolates, into the ground and infiltrates its way into rocks to form groundwater.

Groundwater also flows downhill beneath the surface, and empties into lakes and seas.

Every minute of the day, more than 990 million tons (900 million tons) of water falls to Earth as rain – that's 150 times the weight of the Great Pyramid at Giza, Egypt. This may sound like a lot, but that works out to an average global daily rainfall of just 0.07 inches.

Wet
The wettest place on Earth is Mawsynram, India, with an annual average rainfall of 467.36 inches (11,871 mm).

... and dry
In contrast, the Dry Valleys in Antarctica have no precipitation and scientists believe that it hasn't rained there for nearly 2 million years!

Condensation
Water vapor in the air condenses to form droplets that create clouds.

Transpiration
Plants release water vapor into the air in a process called transpiration.

A single drop of water can take from just nine days to up to 40,000 years to move through the water cycle.

Evaporation
Warmth from the Sun causes water at the surface of seas and lakes to evaporate and turn into water vapor.

The oceans cover some 71 percent of Earth's surface and they range from cold, frozen bodies of water to warm tropical seas.

Pacific Ocean

Area: **62.46 million square miles (161.76 million km sq)**
The Pacific is the world's largest ocean, although it is getting smaller every year as its tectonic plates crash into each other.

On its own,
the Pacific Ocean holds about
**160,000,000
cubic miles**
of water—that's nearly half of all the water in the world's seas and oceans.

Southern Ocean

Area: **8.48 million square miles (21.96 million sq km)**
Surrounding the continent of Antarctica, this ocean has some of the strongest winds on the planet and, while large parts are frozen through winter, the summer months see it teem with life.

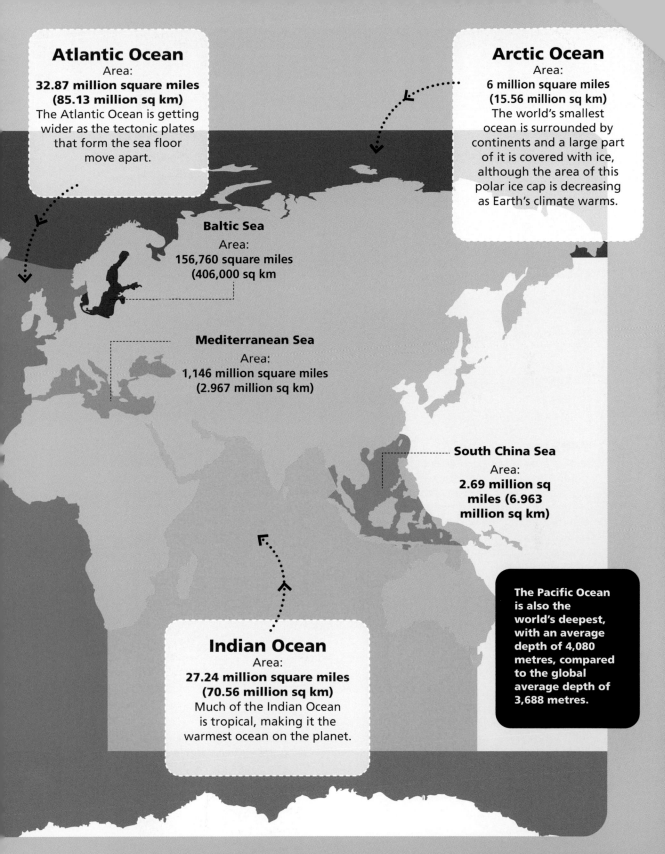

Atlantic Ocean
Area:
**32.87 million square miles
(85.13 million sq km)**
The Atlantic Ocean is getting
wider as the tectonic plates
that form the sea floor
move apart.

Arctic Ocean
Area:
**6 million square miles
(15.56 million sq km)**
The world's smallest
ocean is surrounded by
continents and a large part
of it is covered with ice,
although the area of this
polar ice cap is decreasing
as Earth's climate warms.

Baltic Sea
Area:
**156,760 square miles
(406,000 sq km**

Mediterranean Sea
Area:
**1,146 million square miles
(2.967 million sq km)**

South China Sea
Area:
**2.69 million sq
miles (6.963
million sq km)**

The Pacific Ocean
is also the
world's deepest,
with an average
depth of 4,080
metres, compared
to the global
average depth of
3,688 metres.

Indian Ocean
Area:
**27.24 million square miles
(70.56 million sq km)**
Much of the Indian Ocean
is tropical, making it the
warmest ocean on the planet.

The water in Earth's seas and oceans is always on the move as waves push the water up and down, while deep below the surface, huge currents drive water around the entire planet.

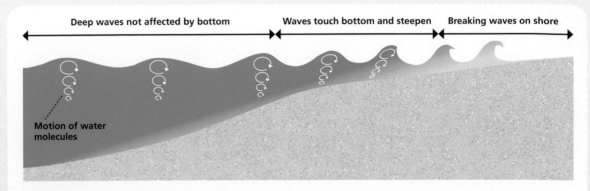

Deep waves not affected by bottom | Waves touch bottom and steepen | Breaking waves on shore

Motion of water molecules

Making waves

Waves are caused by energy passing through the water and they are usually formed when wind blows over the water's surface. The friction between the moving air and the water causes a circular motion in the water as energy is transmitted through the water—the water itself doesn't travel very far. When the wave reaches the shore, the decrease in the water's depth causes the bottom of the wave to slow down and compress, pushing the top, or crest, of the wave up. Before long, the wave topples over, crashing down onto the shore.

Brazilian surfer Rodrigo Koxa holds the record for the largest wave ever surfed:

79.99 feet (24.38 m) tall

off the coast of Nazaré, Portugal in November 2017.

Up from the deep

In places close to coastlines, prevailing winds can push surface waters away from the shore. In their place, cooler waters from the deep ocean well up. These are usually rich in nutrients and their appearance can trigger a bloom in microscopic plankton which, in turn, attracts huge amounts of other sea life.

On the surface

Ocean winds usually blow from the same direction, and these prevailing winds push surface waters around the oceans, forming large circular currents known as gyres. These gyres push cold water from the poles toward the equator and carry warm tropical water toward the poles.

- - - Warm current
- - - Cold current
- - - Neutral current

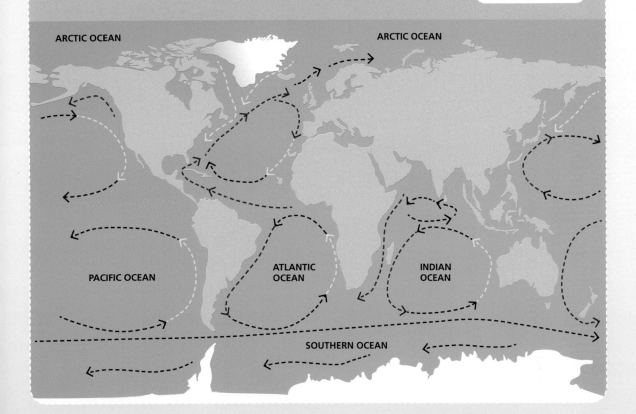

ARCTIC OCEAN

ARCTIC OCEAN

PACIFIC OCEAN

ATLANTIC OCEAN

INDIAN OCEAN

SOUTHERN OCEAN

Conveyor belt

The movement of the waters is linked in one giant current or conveyor belt that runs right through all of Earth's oceans. This features cold currents deep below the surface that well up in some places, such as the northern Pacific, to become warmer surface currents. This global ocean conveyor belt of water can take hundreds of years to complete a circuit of the globe.

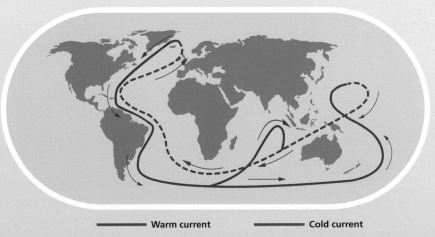

Warm current   Cold current

WHERE SEA MEETS LAND

The never-ending pounding of waves against the shore batters rocks and stones, creating a range of coastal formations from flat, sandy beaches to towering cliffs, stacks, and arches.

Coastal features

Waves that hit a beach at an angle will push sand and shingle along the coast, stripping one part of the shore and dumping it elsewhere. This process is called longshore drift and it can form bars that stretch out into and may even enclose the mouth of a river or bay. On one side of the bar is the sea, while the other side surrounds a body of water called a lagoon. Long strips of beach that stretch out into the ocean are called spits.

Forming sand

When a wave hits the shore, it can apply a pressure of thousands of pounds per square yard. This force can smash apart rocks, dragging them away and grinding them against other stones and debris. Over time, large stones are broken down into smaller and smaller pieces, from pebbles to shingle and, finally, tiny grains of sand.

Tall cliffs are formed where the sea cuts away at the rock, creating a platform of debris at the base of the cliff. In some places, the rock may be softer and the waves cut out caves and arches from these weaker locations. When an arch collapses, it leaves behind a tower of rock in the water, called a stack.

Living with tides

The daily movement of the tides floods coastal areas for parts of the day and leaves them exposed for the rest of the time. This changeable environment can be a tough place to live, but many species of plant and animal have made these places their homes. Seaweeds, small crabs, and fish and anemones can be found in tidal pools that are left behind when the tide is out, while some grasses can cope with the salty conditions found in coastal salt marshes. When the tide is out, many sea birds walk over the exposed ground, feeding on worms and shellfish hiding under the sand.

Sandpipers have long legs to wade through any shallow water left by the retreating tide, and long bills to pick invertebrates out from the mud and sand.

Some parts of the coast may be formed of a tougher rock which does not erode so quickly. These harder areas will form headlands that stick out into sea, while the softer areas on either side will be eroded away by the sea to form bays and inlets.

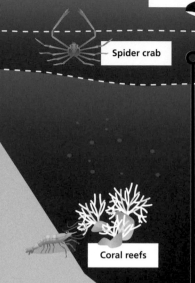

Orca

Spider crab

Coral reefs

Below the surface, Earth's oceans change as you travel down through them. Sunlight soon disappears, temperatures drop, and pressures can increase to crushing extremes.

Surface Zone

This is the smallest zone and only stretches down to about 660 feet (200 m), making up just 5 percent of the average ocean depth. The topmost areas are fully lit at midday, and this is usually the warmest zone, but temperatures can vary depending on surface conditions and the location.

Twilight Zone

This zone forms about 20 percent of the average ocean depth and stretches from about 660–3300 feet (200–1,000 m). Little sunlight reaches the top part of this zone and the lower parts are completely dark.

Deep Ocean

The largest part of the oceans, this zone makes up about 75 percent of the average ocean depth, stretching below 3,300 feet (1,000 m) to the ocean floor. This zone is completely dark and pressures are more than 100 times greater than at the surface, while temperatures are just above freezing.

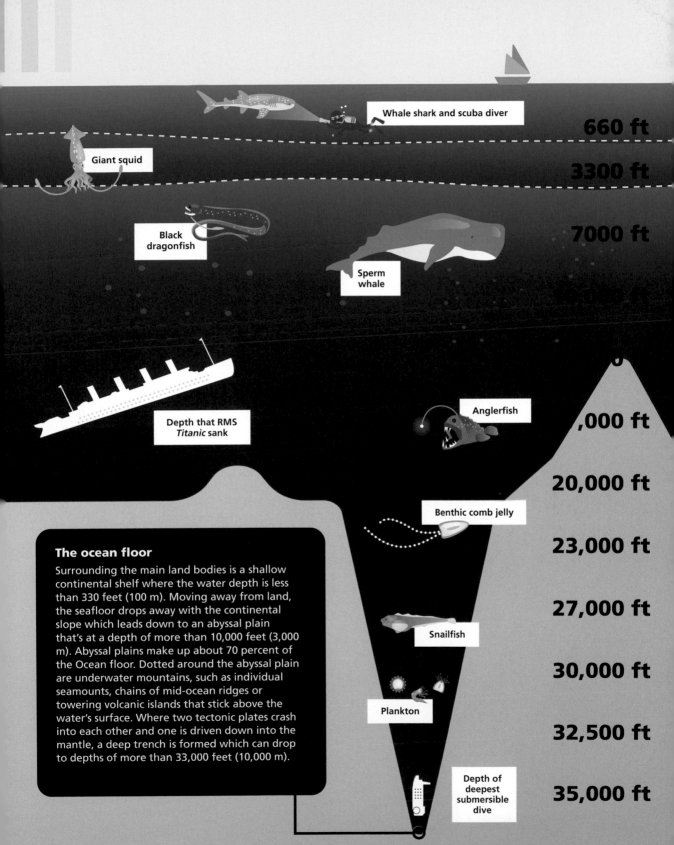

Whale shark and scuba diver

660 ft

Giant squid

3300 ft

Black dragonfish

7000 ft

Sperm whale

Depth that RMS *Titanic* sank

Anglerfish

,000 ft

20,000 ft

Benthic comb jelly

23,000 ft

The ocean floor

Surrounding the main land bodies is a shallow continental shelf where the water depth is less than 330 feet (100 m). Moving away from land, the seafloor drops away with the continental slope which leads down to an abyssal plain that's at a depth of more than 10,000 feet (3,000 m). Abyssal plains make up about 70 percent of the Ocean floor. Dotted around the abyssal plain are underwater mountains, such as individual seamounts, chains of mid-ocean ridges or towering volcanic islands that stick above the water's surface. Where two tectonic plates crash into each other and one is driven down into the mantle, a deep trench is formed which can drop to depths of more than 33,000 feet (10,000 m).

Snailfish

27,000 ft

30,000 ft

Plankton

32,500 ft

Depth of deepest submersible dive

35,000 ft

Water falls from the sky as rain, snow, and hail. Once on the ground, it flows downhill, joining together to form streams and rivers that flow toward the sea, shaping the land as they flow through it.

River course
As a river flows toward the sea, it will carve a path, or course, through the countryside.

Upper course
The start of a river is called its source. This could be a spring (where water wells up from underground) or it could be a patch of saturated ground. The water collects to form a channel that flows quickly down a steep slope, eroding the banks and floor as it moves. The stream or river will have a small cross-section.

Lower course
As it nears the end of its journey, the river will be at its widest and the slope at its shallowest. It will deposit most of its sediment during this stage.

River features

During its upper course, a river will form steep-sided valleys, waterfalls, and gorges. Throughout its middle course, a river will form wider shallower valleys, meanders, and oxbow lakes.

Oxbow lakes form when a river drops so much sediment that it blocks off a river bend, or meander. In its lower course, a river will form wide, flat valleys, sometimes with floodplains, and river deltas.

Longest rivers

4,130 miles (6,650 km)	Nile
3,975 miles (6,400 km)	Amazon-Ucyalo-Apurimac
3,915 miles (6,300 km)	Yangtze
3,710 miles (5,971 km)	Mississippi-Missouri-Red Rock
3,442 miles (5,540 km)	Yenisey-Baikal-Selenga
3,393 miles (5,465 km)	Huang He (Yellow)
3,362 miles (5,410 km)	Ob-Irtysh
3032 miles (4,880 km)	Paraná

Middle course

Farther downstream, the steepness of the river slope will usually decrease and the river will get bigger as it is joined by other streams and rivers. The river will start to drop some of the sediments, forming bends or meanders in its path.

Deltas

Deltas are formed where a river meets the sea and drops any sediment it is carrying faster than the sea can remove it. This sediment builds up to create small islands and channels at the mouth of the river.

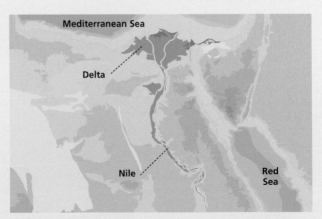

The Nile River forms a triangular-shaped delta where it empties into the Mediterranean Sea.

Plunging down a sheer drop, waterfalls send huge amounts of water crashing down into the riverbed below, carving new land forms in the process.

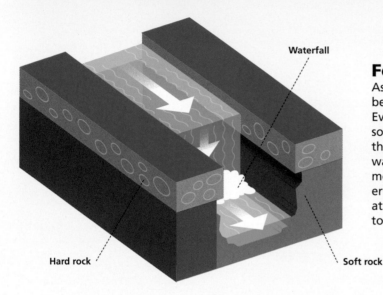

Waterfall

Hard rock

Soft rock

Formation

As a river flows it erodes its sides and bed, cutting down through the rock. Eventually, it may erode down to a softer layer of rock and start carving though this at a faster rate, forming a waterfall. Alternatively, tectonic movements, earthquakes, and volcanic eruptions can push the ground upward at a fault, creating a drop for the river to fall over.

Tallest falls

Angel Falls in Venezuela is the tallest waterfall in the world on land. It drops a total of 1900 feet (979 m), nearly 50 times greater than the height of Niagara Falls. In the Denmark Strait between Greenland and Iceland is an underwater waterfall that is almost 11,483 feet (3,500 m) tall. About 123.6 million cubic feet (3.5 million cubic meters) of cooler water flows over these falls—that's more than 2,000 times the flow that goes over Niagara Falls.

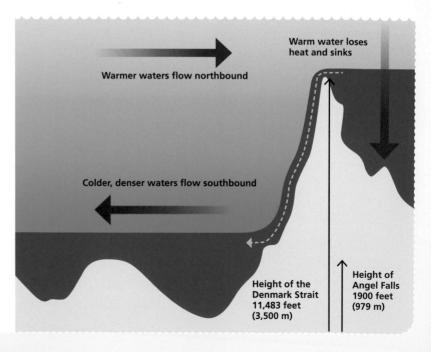

Warm water loses heat and sinks

Warmer waters flow northbound

Colder, denser waters flow southbound

Height of the Denmark Strait 11,483 feet (3,500 m)

Height of Angel Falls 1900 feet (979 m)

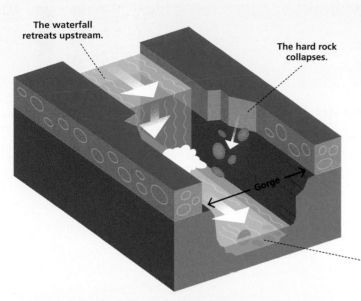

The waterfall retreats upstream.

The hard rock collapses.

Gorge

Debris

Carving a gorge

As a waterfall carves out the softer rock at its base, it produces an overhang, which, eventually, becomes unstable and crashes down. The waterfall will continue this process, called headward erosion, carving out a steep-sided gorge in the process.

MOST POWERFUL LAND WATERFALLS

Inga Falls (DR Congo)
910,024 cubic feet (25,768 cubic m) per second

Livingstone Falls (DR Congo and Congo)
884,986 cubic feet (25,060 cubic m) per second

Boyoma Falls (DR Congo)
599,996 cubic feet (16,990 cubic m) per second

Khone Phapheng Falls (Laos)
56,856 cubic feet (1,610 cubic m) per second

Pará Falls (Venezuela)
125,014 cubic feet (3,540 cubic metres) per second

Victoria falls

Found on the Zambezi River on the border between Zambia and Zimbabwe, Victoria Falls has a drop of 354 feet (108 m) and a width of more than 5,577 feet (1,700 m). The huge amount of water that pours over the edge crashes to the ground with a powerful roar and a towering cloud of spray that can be seen far away, giving the falls its local name of *Mosi-oa-Tunya* ('The Smoke that Thunders').

Lakes are patches of water that have formed in natural basins and are completely surrounded by land. They can range in size from small pools to huge bodies of water that cover thousands of square miles.

Forming lakes
Lakes' basins are formed in various ways. These include:

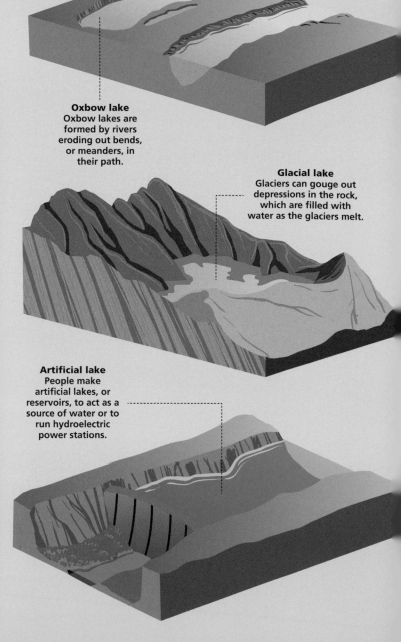

Oxbow lake
Oxbow lakes are formed by rivers eroding out bends, or meanders, in their path.

Glacial lake
Glaciers can gouge out depressions in the rock, which are filled with water as the glaciers melt.

Artificial lake
People make artificial lakes, or reservoirs, to act as a source of water or to run hydroelectric power stations.

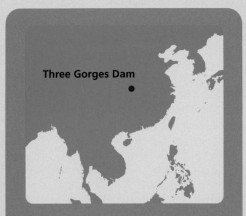

Three Gorges Dam

Three Gorges Dam reservoir
Construction of the Three Gorges Dam in China created a huge artificial lake that stretches for about 375 miles (600 km) upstream behind the dam, flooding valleys and making nearly 1.5 million people leave their homes which were submerged beneath the rising waters. The reservoir provides water to produce some 22,500 megawatts of electricity, making the dam one of the most productive hydroelectric power stations on the planet.

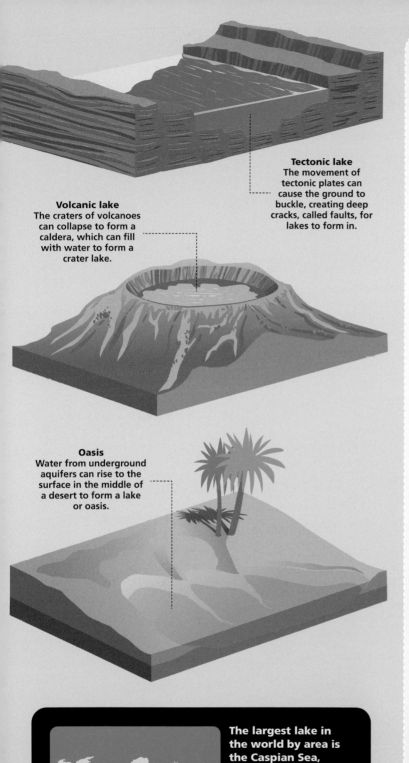

Tectonic lake
The movement of tectonic plates can cause the ground to buckle, creating deep cracks, called faults, for lakes to form in.

Volcanic lake
The craters of volcanoes can collapse to form a caldera, which can fill with water to form a crater lake.

Oasis
Water from underground aquifers can rise to the surface in the middle of a desert to form a lake or oasis.

The largest lake in the world by area is the Caspian Sea, which sits between Europe and Asia. It covers more than 143,000 square miles (370,000 sq km).

Caspian Sea

Lake Baikal

Lake Baikal

Located in Siberia, Russia, Lake Baikal is the oldest lake in the world, having been formed between 20–25 million years ago. It is also the deepest lake on the planet, with a maximum depth of 5,315 feet (1,620 m) – that's deep enough to submerge two Burj Khalifa's, the world's tallest building! In fact, it's so deep that the lake holds about one-fifth of all the planet's surface freshwater—some 5,518 cubic miles (23,000 cubic km)!

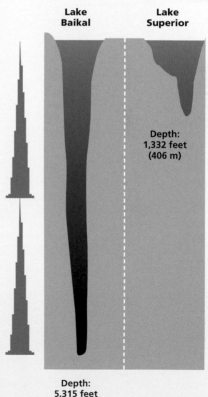

Lake Baikal

Lake Superior

Depth: 1,332 feet (406 m)

Depth: 5,315 feet (1,620 m)

UNDERGROUND WATER AND CAVES

Beneath your feet, huge amounts of water lie buried, trapped by waterproof rocks or slowly moving through the stones and soil before emptying out into rivers, lakes, and the sea.

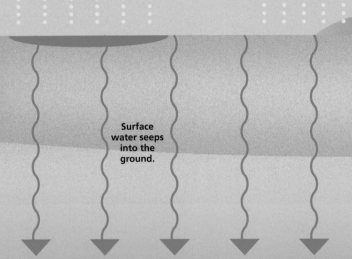

Permeable layer

Surface water seeps into the ground.

Aquifers

Rainwater that falls to the ground will either collect in channels to form streams and rivers or it will seep through the soil and into porous rocks to form underground bodies of water known as aquifers.

One of the largest aquifers sits below the Sahara, covering an area of about 386,000 square miles (1 million square km) beneath Algeria, Tunisia, and Libya.

North-western Saharan Aquifer

Wells, springs, and pumps

Underground water has been a useful source of clean drinkable water for thousands of years. People have dug wells down to reach the water or used pumps to lift the water to the surface. In some places, the water will bubble up to the surface forming a natural spring.

Aquifer

Non-Permeable layer

Permafrost

Groundwater in tundra regions at the poles and high up mountains is usually frozen all year round, creating a solid layer called permafrost.

Permafrost forms a permanently frozen layer just beneath the surface.

Forming caves

Rainwater that falls on regions that have limestone can form huge underground cave networks and caverns. Acids in the rainwater dissolve the limestone rock, eating away at it and carving cracks and caves beneath the ground.

Where water drips from the ceiling it leaves behind small deposits of calcite, which build up over many years to form hanging stalactites. Similarly, water dripping onto the ground causes calcite deposits to build up, forming vertical stalagmites.

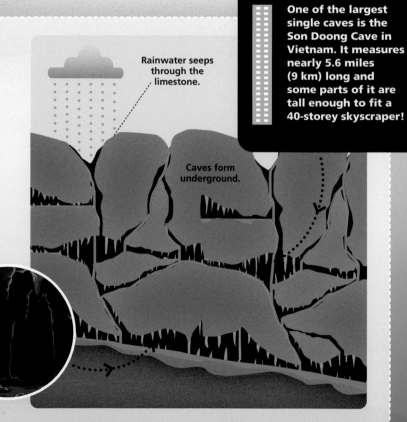

Rainwater seeps through the limestone.

Caves form underground.

One of the largest single caves is the Son Doong Cave in Vietnam. It measures nearly 5.6 miles (9 km) long and some parts of it are tall enough to fit a 40-storey skyscraper!

GLACIERS AND ICE CAPS

Frozen at the planet's poles and at the peaks of its mountains are huge amounts of water that is locked into glaciers and ice caps.

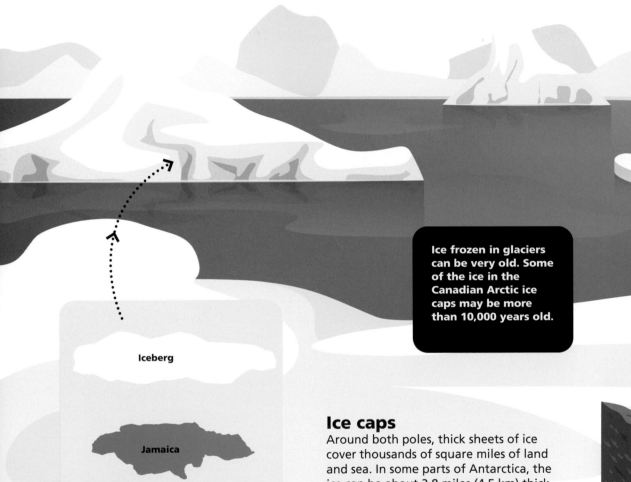

Ice frozen in glaciers can be very old. Some of the ice in the Canadian Arctic ice caps may be more than 10,000 years old.

Iceberg

Jamaica

In March 2000, an iceberg measuring nearly 183 miles (295 km) long and 23 miles (37 km) wide broke off the Antarctic ice sheet. It had a total area of 4,247 square miles (11,000 square km), making it larger than the island of Jamaica.

Ice caps

Around both poles, thick sheets of ice cover thousands of square miles of land and sea. In some parts of Antarctica, the ice can be about 2.8 miles (4.5 km) thick, pushing down on the rock beneath it and causing it to sink into the crust by about 0.6 mile (1 km). At the edges of these ice sheets, warmer conditions cause large pieces of ice called bergs to break away and float off.

Ice ages

As Earth's climate has changed throughout its history, so its polar ice caps have increased and decreased in size, affecting sea levels right around the planet. During the last Ice Age, which ended about 12,000 years ago, glaciers covered about one-third of the land and sea levels were about 395 feet (120 m) lower than they are now.

During the last Ice Age, large woolly mammoths roamed across much of the northern hemisphere.

The Bering Glacier in Alaska, USA, is more than 125 miles (200 km) long, making it the longest glacier on the planet.

Bering Glacier

The main glacier may be joined by other smaller glaciers from side valleys.

Glaciers

Snow that falls on high mountains collects and freezes solid to form glaciers. Even though they are solid, they still flow downhill and are replaced by more snow. These moving sheets of ice pick up rocks and debris from the ground, depositing them elsewhere and scouring out formations in the rock, such as U-shaped valleys, sharp, pointed mountains, and random boulders, called erratics.

In 1953, the Kutiah Glacier in Pakistan grew at a rate of about 367 feet (112 m) every day for three months, covering a total of some 12 miles (7.5 km).

The glacier carves out a U-shaped valley as it moves forward.

CHAPTER 5

THE ATMOSPHERE

THE AIR WE BREATHE

Look outside your window and you will see the atmosphere in action. You can't see the gases that make up the atmosphere, but you can see their effects, from the clouds in the sky to the people, plants, and animals that depend on it.

Air for life

The atmosphere is vital for living things around the planet. It contains the gases they absorb or breathe in and use to produce the energy they need to survive.

The weather

The swirling atmosphere creates the weather we experience as it moves bodies of cold and warm air around, transporting large amounts of water in the form of vapor. This weather could be a cloudless sunny day or it may involve dark, towering clouds that could bring a thunderstorm.

Other worlds

Of the eight planets and more than 200 moons in the Solar System, only a handful have atmospheres. These atmospheres are very different from the one around Earth. For example, Venus has an atmosphere that is 96 percent carbon dioxide, with average temperatures of 867°F (464°C) and clouds of sulfuric acid, while the atmosphere around Mars is very thin, with 95 percent carbon dioxide and an average temperature of -81.4°F (-63°C).

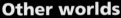

THE ATMOSPHERE'S STRUCTURE

The atmosphere is a thin blanket of gases that surrounds Earth. It protects us from harmful solar rays, keeps us warm by trapping the Sun's energy, and its moving currents provide us with our daily weather.

Troposphere

The lowest and thinnest layer is the troposphere, which stretches up from the surface to an altitude of about 9 miles (14.5 km). The troposphere is the densest layer of the atmosphere, and it contains about 75 percent of all the mass of the atmosphere and about 99 percent of all its water vapor. Because the air is heated by Earth's surface, which is warmed by the Sun, temperatures start to drop as you climb higher through the troposphere.

Stratosphere

Above the troposphere is the stratosphere, which stretches up to an altitude of about 31 miles (50 km). Unlike the troposphere, the temperatures actually increase as you climb higher through the stratosphere, because the air here is heated by ultraviolet radiation from the Sun. The stratosphere contains the ozone layer, which protects us from the Sun's harmful ultraviolet radiation. It's also the highest part of the atmosphere where jet aircraft can fly.

Mesosphere

Above the stratosphere is the mesosphere, the coldest layer in the atmosphere where temperatures drop to -120°F (-85°C). It stretches up to an altitude of about 53 miles (85 km). Noctilucent clouds, the highest to form in the atmosphere, can be found here. It's also the region where most meteors burn up, forming shooting stars in the night sky.

Temperatures in the upper atmosphere can reach

3,600°F (2,000°C).

The edge of space

Most scientists mark the beginning of space at an altitude of 62 miles (100 km), known as the Karman line. Some 99.99997 percent of Earth's atmosphere sits below this line.

Thermosphere

The thermosphere stretches up to an altitude of 360 miles (600 km) and it contains the glowing lights of the aurorae in the southern and northern skies. The International Space Station orbits in this layer of the atmosphere.

Exosphere

The outermost layer of the atmosphere is the exosphere, which fades off to an altitude of about 6,200 miles (10,000 km).

The atmosphere is made up of a cocktail of different gases and tiny particles, and while some of these are very important to life on Earth, too much of some of them can create problems.

Content of air

The atmosphere is a mixture of different gases and particles.

78 percent is made up of nitrogen.

1 percent is made up of other gases, including argon, hydrogen, neon, and carbon dioxide.

21 percent is made up of oxygen.

The atmosphere contains lots of tiny particles, which are called aerosols. These particles include dust, smoke, soot, car exhaust fumes, and pollen.

Oxygen is vital for all living things on the planet. They use oxygen to produce energy in a process called respiration, releasing carbon dioxide in the process.

The atmosphere also holds water vapor. The amount of vapor depends on the humidity of the conditions.

Carbon dioxide is also important for many living things. Plants use carbon dioxide to produce sugars, in a process called photosynthesis. However, too much carbon dioxide in the air can cause problems, leading to increased temperatures and global warming.

Tiny living things are also found living and floating in the air. These mini organisms are called bioaerosols.

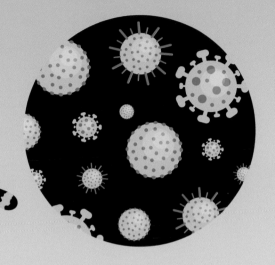

Blue skies

Light from the Sun contains all the colors of the rainbow, which, when mixed together, appear as white light. The mixture of molecules in Earth's atmosphere scatters these rainbow colors, but blue is scattered more than any other. This is why we see the sky as blue for most of the time.

Sunrise and sunset

When the Sun is low in the sky, close to sunrise or sunset, its light has to travel through more of the atmosphere before it reaches your eyes. Even more of the blue light is scattered, leaving reds and yellows to travel straight to your eyes, making sunrises and sunsets appear red or orange in color.

Earth's atmosphere is constantly on the move, as the Sun's heat warms the planet and the air above it. This movement produces huge currents of swirling air, giving us our wind and weather.

Warmth from the Sun

Energy from the Sun warms the Earth and the warm surface heats the air above it. This warmer air rises high into the atmosphere, where it spreads out, cools, and sinks back down to the surface, where it will be warmed again. This process produces large, circular convection currents of air.

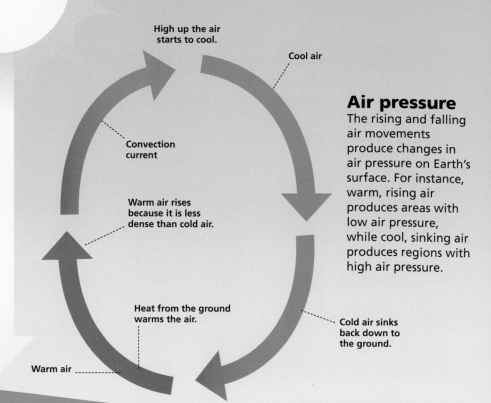

High up the air starts to cool.

Cool air

Convection current

Warm air rises because it is less dense than cold air.

Heat from the ground warms the air.

Warm air

Cold air sinks back down to the ground.

Air pressure

The rising and falling air movements produce changes in air pressure on Earth's surface. For instance, warm, rising air produces areas with low air pressure, while cool, sinking air produces regions with high air pressure.

This circular movement is called a convection current and we feel this air movement as wind.

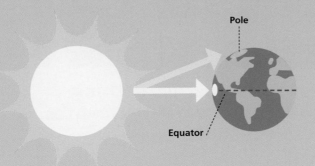

Warmer than others

Because Earth is a sphere and not flat, a region close to the equator receives more of the Sun's energy than a similar-sized region that is close to the poles. This is why it is warmer at the equator than it is at the poles.

Some parts of the planet are covered with water, while others have land. Land usually heats up and cools down more quickly than water, creating a further unbalance. Also, some areas of land absorb more of the Sun's energy than others. For example, dark soil absorbs more energy and so warms the air, while snow-covered areas reflect a lot of the Sun's energy without absorbing it.

80 percent

100 percent

10 percent

Snow—high albedo

Dark soil—low albedo

Coriolis effect

Earth spins once on its axis every 24 hours. This pushes moving air off a straight course. North of the equator, air is pushed so that it swerves to the right, while south of the equator, air is pushed to the left. This is called the Coriolis effect.

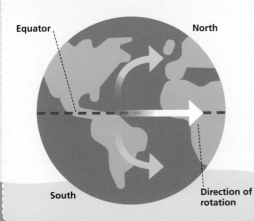

Equator

North

South

Direction of rotation

Jet streams

About 7.5 miles (12 km) above Earth's surface, strong currents of air form where cold and warm air masses meet. These are known as jet streams, and they usually reach between 80–140 miles (129–225 km) per hour, although they can be much faster than this. Jet aircraft use jet streams to push them along faster so that they arrive at their destinations earlier.

CLIMATE

Differences in the amount of Sun's energy reaching the surface, and other factors, create varying climates around the planet. These affect the long-term conditions in different places.

Weather and climate

The weather is the short-term conditions experienced at a place. So, one day it may be sunny, but the next day could have rain. The climate of a place refers to the conditions experienced there over a long period of time.

Climate zones

Earth has five major climate zones:

Tropical—the regions closest to the equator are the warmest. Rising currents of warm air produce huge storm clouds that drop their moisture in heavy tropical storms. These conditions are ideal for tropical rainforests to thrive.

Dry—these areas are usually found where dry descending air produces few clouds and very little rainfall. For example, there are parts of the Atacama Desert in South America where no rain has fallen for 400 years.

Temperate—these regions usually have warm summers and cold winters, and rain can fall here at any time during the year.

Continental—these areas are found in the center of the large northern continents and they usually have long, cold winters followed by mild summers.

Polar—found around the poles, these areas are cold all year round.

CLIMATE CHANGE

Earth's average temperatures have risen over the last 100 years as human activity has increased the levels of greenhouse gases, such as carbon dioxide, in the air. This increase in temperature could benefit some but cause suffering to others.

Rising temperatures
Since the later 19th century, Earth's average temperature has increased by 2°F (1.1°C), and will continue to rise unless people stop adding greenhouse gases to the atmosphere. This rise in temperature affects people and animals around the world.

Growing seasons
Some parts of the world will see a longer growing season. Warmer conditions will reduce the amount of frost, providing farmers with more days to grow crops. In the US, the length of the growing season could increase by eight weeks in some parts of the country.

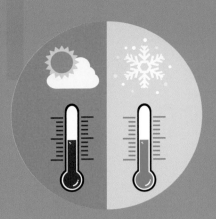

More rain

Warmer weather could bring more rain to some places. Other regions may experience drought, with extreme heat days increasing from happening once every 20 years to once every 2–3 years in the US.

Extreme weather events

Extreme weather events will increase in their severity and number. Since the 1980s, the number of the highest categories of hurricanes has increased and will continue to do so as the climate warms.

Melting ice

By the middle of this century, the Arctic will become completely ice-free during the summer months. Sea levels will rise by 8.2 feet (2.5 m) by the year 2100, flooding low-lying coasts and many islands.

Decline in sea life

As water temperatures increase and levels of carbon dioxide rise, sea waters will become more acidic, leading to a decline in sea life. An increase in sea temperatures of 2.7°F (1.5°C) would see coral reefs decline by between 70–90 percent.

THE SEASONS

As Earth orbits the Sun, it is slightly tilted to one side. One half points toward the Sun for one part of the year, and then points away six months later. This creates the seasons.

Around the Sun

Earth is tilted by 23.5 degrees in relation to the Sun.

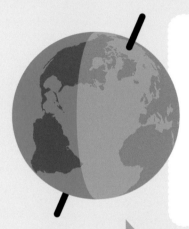

June

The northern hemisphere is pointing toward the Sun, so it receives more of the Sun's energy, making it summer here and winter in the southern hemisphere.

Changing conditions

The changes in the seasons bring a change in weather conditions. In the spring, the weather starts to get warmer and trees start to grow leaves. In the summer, the weather is usually its warmest and trees are in full bloom. In the autumn, the weather starts to cool and tree leaves turn brown and drop off. In the winter, the weather is at its coolest, the trees are without their leaves, and they are usually dormant.

Changing days

Earth's tilt also means that the lengths of daylight alter throughout the year.

Around June 21st, the northern hemisphere has its longest day, while the southern hemisphere has its shortest day. The longest day is known as the summer solstice.

Around December 21st, the northern hemisphere has its shortest day, while the southern hemisphere has its longest day. The shortest day is known as the winter solstice.

Around March 21st and September 21st, days and nights are equal lengths in both northern and southern hemispheres. These are known as the equinoxes.

Tropical seasons

The tropical regions only have two different seasons during the year. As the tropical rain belt moves up and down across the equator, it causes a dry season without rain and a wet season with lots of rainfall.

March

The Earth is side on to the Sun and it is autumn in the southern hemisphere and spring in the northern hemisphere.

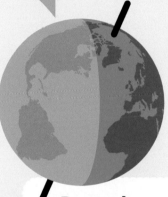

December

The southern hemisphere is pointing towards the Sun, so it receives more of the Sun's energy, making it summer here and winter in the northern hemisphere.

September

The Earth is side on to the Sun and it is autumn in the northern hemisphere and spring in the southern hemisphere.

During the northern hemisphere summer, parts around the North Pole experience 24 hours of daylight...

... while parts near the South Pole experience 24 hours of darkness. This is reversed six months later.

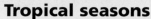

Warm wet air over the tropical regions can build up to create the most powerful storms on the planet. Known as tropical cyclones, they are called different names depending where they start, including hurricanes, typhoons, and cyclones.

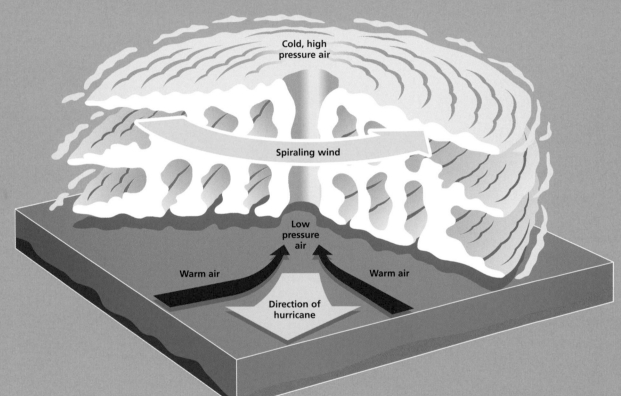

Cold, high pressure air

Spiraling wind

Low pressure air

Warm air

Warm air

Direction of hurricane

Swirling vortex

As the warm humid air builds up, it starts to rotate. Clouds build up and so does the wind speed, until it reaches 74 miles (119 km) and the storm becomes a tropical cyclone. It usually has a spiral of thick clouds that swirls around a relatively calm, clear area, called the eye.

Storm categories

Tropical cyclones are classed according to their wind speeds.

Category 1—74–95 miles (119–153 km) per hour
Category 2—96–110 (154–110 km) per hour
Category 3—111–129 miles (178-208 km) per hour
Category 4—130–156 miles (209⊠–251 km) per hour
Category 5—more than 156.5 miles (252 km) per hour

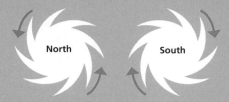

North   South

Clockwise or counterclockwise

The Coriolis effect causes tropical cyclones to spin in different directions, depending on which hemisphere they form in. In the northern hemisphere, the storms rotate counterclockwise, while in the southern hemisphere, the storms rotate clockwise.

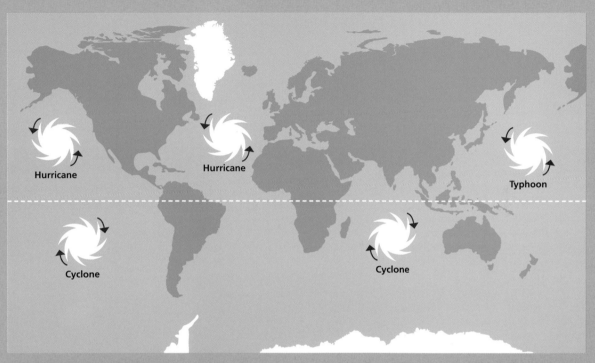

Hurricane

Hurricane

Typhoon

Cyclone

Cyclone

Typhoon Tip was the largest tropical cyclone ever recorded. It formed in October 1979 and grew to measure about 2,220 kilometres across with peak winds reaching 190 miles (305 km) per hour.

Storm names

Tropical storms that form in the North Atlantic and the central and eastern North Pacific are called hurricanes. Those storms that form in the western North Pacific are called typhoons and those that form in the South Pacific and Indian Ocean are called cyclones. Once it becomes a tropical cyclone then it is given a name. These progress in alphabetical order and are usually reused every six years. However, names of really bad storms may be retired completely.

Reaching land

As the storm approaches land, it batters the coast with powerful winds and waves. It also causes a huge storm surge, which is a great mass of water that rushes onto land and causes flooding. As the hurricane moves over land, its power starts to drop as it can no longer pick up any more warm, humid air.

High winds

Storm surge

TORNADOES

Tornadoes are powerful rotating columns of air that move across the countryside, tearing through buildings and leaving huge amounts of damage in their wake.

Thunder cloud

Funnel formation

No one knows exactly how tornadoes form, but they often develop under enormous storm clouds called supercells. These create spinning funnels of air that stretch down to the ground to become tornadoes. Because a tornado is formed from spinning air, it can often be invisible, and is only really "seen" when it has picked up dust debris and water vapor to form a visible funnel or column shape. Inside the rotating column, an area of low pressure creates updrafts of air that create the destruction. Most only last for a few minutes and travel less than 3 miles (5 km). Some, however, can last for several hours and cover more than 93 miles (150 km).

Cold air

Counterclockwise rotation

Side wind

Warm air

Rotating
column of air

Although tornadoes can occur at any time of the day or night, they are most common between 4–9 pm.

Tornado Alley

The United States experiences about 1,200 tornadoes every year, but most of them occur in a region called Tornado Alley. This covers a large area of the central states, such as Texas, Oklahoma, Kansas, South Dakota, Iowa, and Nebraska.

Tornado scales

Meteorologists use the Enhanced Fujita (EF) scale to classify different tornadoes. This rates the fastest speed of a three-second gust of wind in the storm.

	EF number	three-second gust	Damage
	0	65–85 miles (104–137 km) per hour	Minor or no damage
	1	85–110 miles (138–177 km) per hour	Moderate damage
	2	110–135 miles (178–217 km) per hour	Considerable damage
	3	135–165 miles (218–266 km) per hour	Severe damage
	4	165–200 miles (267–322 km) per hour	Extreme damage
	5	More than 200 miles (323 km) kilometres per hour	Total destruction of buildings

The strongest tornadoes can reach wind speeds of up to 300 miles (480 km) per hour and they are strong enough to uproot trees, tear the roof off a building, and throw cars over hundreds of yards. The deadliest tornado recorded occurred in Bangladesh in 1989. It destroyed more than 20 villages and killed around 1,300 people.

Waterspouts

Tornadoes that form over lakes or the sea draw up spinning columns of water, forming waterspouts.

DROUGHT

Droughts are periods when little or no rain falls in a region. They may not have the immediate effects of a hurricane or a tornado, but they cause enormous amounts of damage.

Drought effects

If little rain falls, the soil can dry out and this can kill plants, including crops, if they do not have any other form of irrigation. With few plants to hold the soil together, it becomes cracked and loose and can blow away in strong winds, forming large dust clouds and leaving behind unfertile areas of land where few plants can grow.

Refugees

With little food and water available in a drought-hit area, people who live there are forced to leave in search of something to eat and drink. The very worst droughts can force millions of these refugees to travel hundreds of miles.

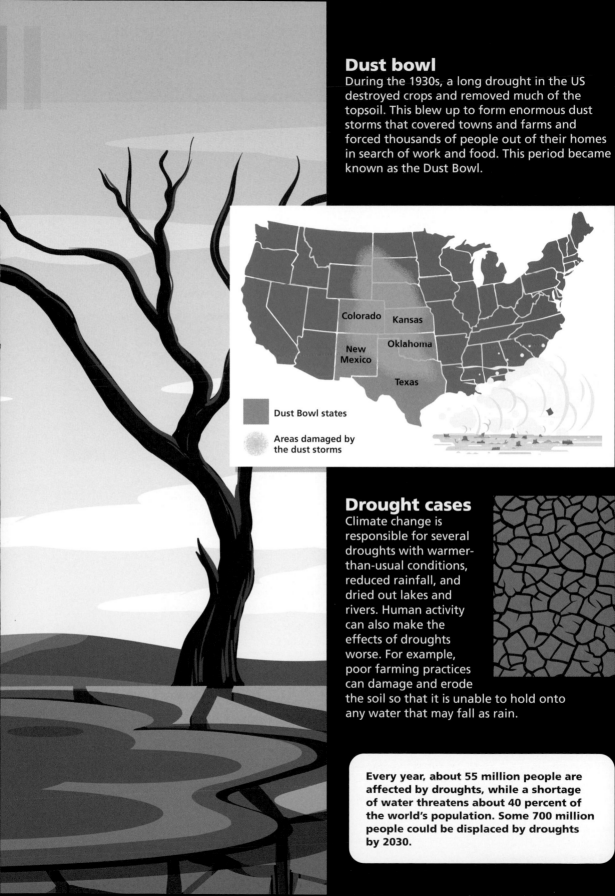

Dust bowl

During the 1930s, a long drought in the US destroyed crops and removed much of the topsoil. This blew up to form enormous dust storms that covered towns and farms and forced thousands of people out of their homes in search of work and food. This period became known as the Dust Bowl.

Colorado Kansas

New Mexico Oklahoma

Texas

Dust Bowl states

Areas damaged by the dust storms

Drought cases

Climate change is responsible for several droughts with warmer-than-usual conditions, reduced rainfall, and dried out lakes and rivers. Human activity can also make the effects of droughts worse. For example, poor farming practices can damage and erode the soil so that it is unable to hold onto any water that may fall as rain.

Every year, about 55 million people are affected by droughts, while a shortage of water threatens about 40 percent of the world's population. Some 700 million people could be displaced by droughts by 2030.

The swirling of the planet's ocean currents can affect the weather conditions in nearby regions. Changes in these patterns can have severe effects on regions, as seen during El Niño climate pattern in the Pacific.

Normal conditions

In normal times, winds blow west across the Pacific, pushing warm water at the surface toward Asia and Australia. This causes cooler waters to upwell, or rise up to the surface along the coast of South America, bringing nutrients with them from the deep. Tiny plankton feed on these nutrients and these attract larger ocean animals, making these waters very good for fishing.

Warmer waters in the western Pacific produce rains around Indonesia and New Guinea, while the cooler waters to the east keep South America relatively dry.

"El Niño" means **"Little Boy" or "Christ Child"** and is so called because it usually takes place around Christmas time.

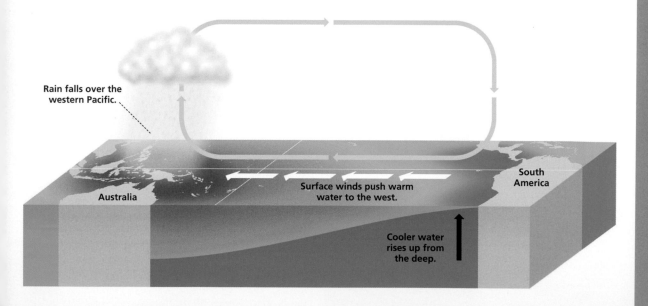

Rain falls over the western Pacific.

Australia

Surface winds push warm water to the west.

South America

Cooler water rises up from the deep.

El Niño

During El Niño, the westward-blowing winds become weaker, and warmer water moves back toward South America. As a result, the cooler waters can't rise up along the South American coast and without the nutrients these bring, many fish cannot survive.

The warmer waters bring increased rainfall in South America which can be torrential, causing terrible flooding. On the other side of the Pacific, a lack of rain can produce droughts.

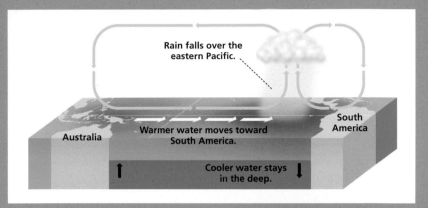

Rain falls over the eastern Pacific.

South America

Australia

Warmer water moves toward South America.

Cooler water stays in the deep.

Global effect

When El Niño is very strong, its effects can be felt much farther away, with fishing catches being affected as far north as Alaska and storms hammering the west coast of the United States and warm winters in the Midwest of the country. It can also affect the seasonal monsoons in the Indian Ocean and has even increased rainfall during the rainy season in Africa.

El Niño and La Niña events occur every two to seven years and last for **nine to twelve months.**

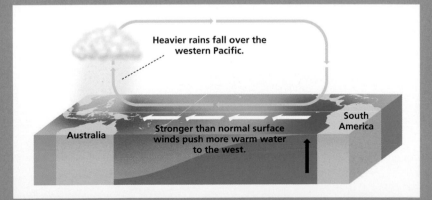

Heavier rains fall over the western Pacific.

South America

Australia

Stronger than normal surface winds push more warm water to the west.

La Niña

La Niña is a climate event that has the opposite effects to El Niño. It features stronger westward-blowing winds, pushing more warm water toward Asia and Australia, while making the waters of the coast of South America even colder.

CHAPTER 6

LIVING PLANET

Earth holds a special place in the Universe because it is the only place we know of that supports life. A vast range of living organisms exist here across a diverse range of habitats from the frozen poles to the scorching regions of the tropics.

What is a habitat?

A habitat is the place where an organism lives. The habitat supplies the organism with everything it needs to survive, including water, food, enough space to live, and somewhere to shelter. The availability of each of these can affect how an organism behaves or looks.

A region's particular habitat depends on the climate it has and its position on the planet. Conditions nearer the equator are warmer than those closer to the poles, while the amount of rainfall a region receives determines whether it can support a rich forest or an arid desert habitat.

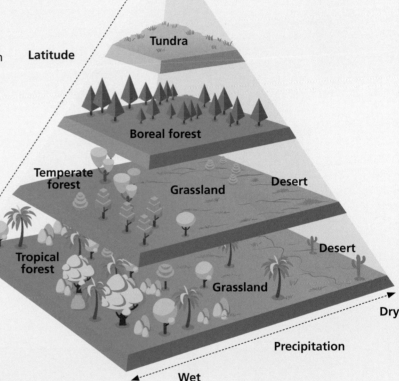

Pole

Latitude

Tundra

Boreal forest

Temperate forest

Grassland

Desert

Desert

Tropical forest

Grassland

Equator

Dry

Precipitation

Wet

Adaptations

If an organism is adapted to live in a particular habitat, then it is more likely to survive. For example, conifer trees have a triangular shape, which stops too much snow building up on them, so they are better adapted to live in cold habitats than deciduous trees. Animals that live in colder habitats are adapted to the conditions there. A musk ox has a thick coat of hair to keep it warm on the Arctic tundra.

DESERTS

Deserts are places with very little rainfall. These dry regions of the world may look like places where nothing can live, but plenty of plants and animals thrive in the conditions found there.

Hot and dry deserts or arid deserts—these have warm and dry conditions all year round. They include the Sahara in North Africa and the Mojave in North America.

Semi-arid deserts—these are a little cooler than hot, dry deserts, with long hot summers and cooler winters that may have some rain. This type of desert can be found in Greenland, North America, Europe, and Asia.

Coastal deserts—these have thick fogs that roll in from the sea, but very little rain. They include the Atacama Desert in South America.

Cold deserts—have very low temperatures all year round, but they are still very dry. The largest desert in the world is the cold desert of Antarctica.

Living in deserts

Plants and animals that live in the desert have body adaptations to help them survive in the harsh conditions.

Cactus

A thick skin that feels waxy reflects the sun's heat and reduces water loss. A thick fleshy stem stores water. Spikes covering the stem and leaves stop animals eating the plant. Long roots tap water that's deep underground.

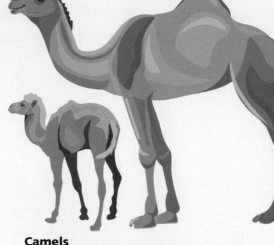

Camels

Wide feet stop the camel from sinking into the sand. Long eyelashes, hairy ears, and an ability to close the nostrils keep out sand. They can go for more than a week without drinking. Their humps store fat, so they can go for long periods without eating.

MAJOR DESERTS

Antarctic desert (Antarctica)
5.48 million square miles (14.2 million sq km)

Arctic Desert (North America, northern Europe and Asia)
5.37 million square miles (13.9 million sq km)

Sahara (North Africa)
3.55 million square miles (9.2 million sq km)

Arabian Desert (Western Asia)
900,000 square miles (2.33 million sq km)

Gobi Desert (Eastern Asia)
500,000 square miles (1.295 million sq km)

Kalahari Desert (Southern Africa)
347,000 square miles (900,000 sq km)

Namib Desert (Southern Africa)
62,000 square miles (160,000 sq km)

FORESTS

Forest habitats around the world differ depending on the climate over the course of the year.

Tropical forest

Tropical rainforests are found close to the equator where conditions are warm and wet all year round. The trees growing in these forests, such as mahogany and ebony, have large broad leaves that block out much of the light, leaving the forest floor dark and shaded. The thick plant coverage grows in a number of layers.

Emergents —some extra-tall trees grow above the main canopy.

Main canopy— where the leaves and branches of most of the trees are found.

Understory—this is made up of shrubs and small trees.

Forest floor—few plants survive here as little light reaches this zone.

The Amazon rainforest is home to about **10 percent** of all known species on Earth and covers about **40 percent** of the entire South American continent.

Boreal forest

Stretching right across the north of Asia, Europe, and North America is a huge band of cold boreal forest. Winters here are long and cold, while summers can be mild but very short. Trees that grow here, such as firs and pine, have needle-like waxy leaves that stay on the tree all year.

Temperate forest

Temperate forests are found in regions between the tropics and the polar regions. Winters here can be cold, but summers are warm. These forests contain a mix of evergreen trees and deciduous ones that drop their leaves in autumn before growing them again in spring.

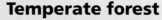

Temperate rainforests

Temperate rainforests are found in cooler parts of the world that receive a lot of rain, such as the coast of northwest North America and New Zealand. The forests can contain either evergreen or deciduous trees, while the forest floor is covered with small shrubs as well as mosses and ferns.

GRASSLANDS

At the heart of all of the continents are enormous areas of land that are dominated by grasses. They are found in both temperate and tropical parts of the world and many of them are home to huge herds of grazing animals that feed on the grasses.

Grass

Grass is a very tough plant that can survive the drier conditions found in the center of continents. These drier conditions prevent trees forming large forests. Grasses can also survive periods of drought as well as flooding, freezing conditions, fires, and grazing by animals. The grass plants grow from near or below the ground, so they are unaffected when their tops are chewed off by a grazing animal.

Tropical grasslands

Found in regions that are close to the equator, these areas have two seasons—wet and dry. Plants and animals that live here have to cope with long periods of drought, so have either adapted to store enough water to survive the dry periods or they will migrate to another region where rains are falling.

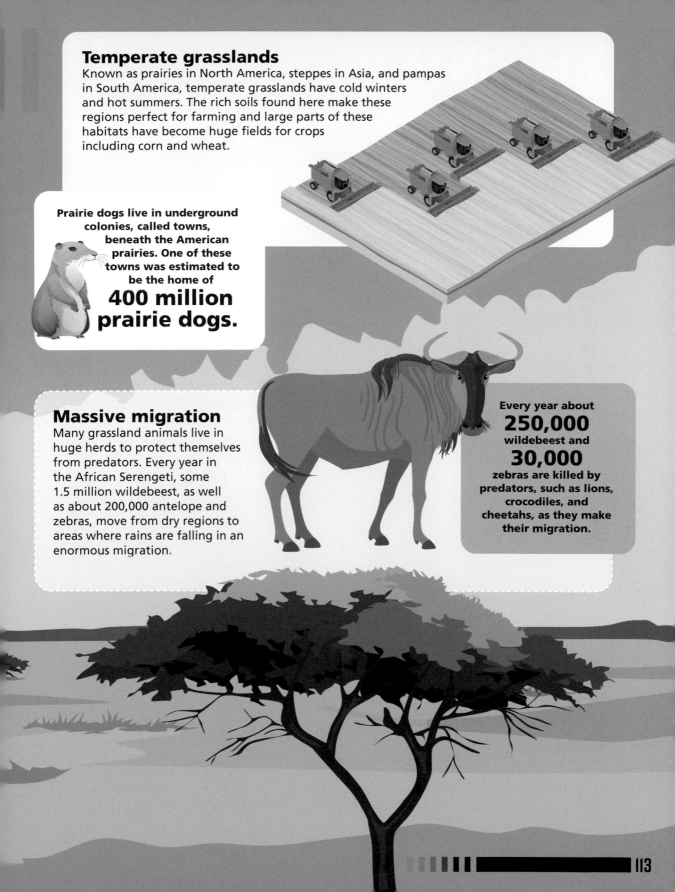

Temperate grasslands

Known as prairies in North America, steppes in Asia, and pampas in South America, temperate grasslands have cold winters and hot summers. The rich soils found here make these regions perfect for farming and large parts of these habitats have become huge fields for crops including corn and wheat.

Prairie dogs live in underground colonies, called towns, beneath the American prairies. One of these towns was estimated to be the home of **400 million prairie dogs.**

Massive migration

Many grassland animals live in huge herds to protect themselves from predators. Every year in the African Serengeti, some 1.5 million wildebeest, as well as about 200,000 antelope and zebras, move from dry regions to areas where rains are falling in an enormous migration.

Every year about **250,000** wildebeest and **30,000** zebras are killed by predators, such as lions, crocodiles, and cheetahs, as they make their migration.

MOUNTAINS

Formed when Earth's tectonic plates slam into each other or from the eruptions of powerful volcanoes, mountains are found in long chains that stretch along continents or as isolated peaks that tower above the surrounding land.

Tallest mountains on each continent

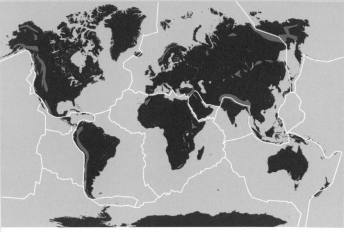

■ Mountain ranges

ASIA
MOUNT EVEREST
29,035 FEET
(8,850 M)

SOUTH AMERICA
ACONCAGUA
22,841 FEET (6,962 M)

NORTH AMERICA
DENALI
20,322 FEET (6,194 M)

EUROPE
MOUNT ELBRUS
18,510 FEET (5,642 M)

ANTARCTICA
VINSON MASSIF
16,066 FEET (4,897 M)

Altitude zones

As you climb up a mountain the conditions change, creating different zones at different altitudes, each with different plants and animals.

At the base of mountains found in tropical parts of the world are thick rainforests. These give way to evergreen tropical forests, which then lead to deciduous broadleaf forests. Above these are evergreen coniferous forests which mark the end of the trees. Above these are subalpine meadows and treeless alpine meadows, before you reach the mountain tundra. At the very top, snows and glaciers are found all year round, even on mountains at the equator, such as Kilimanjaro.

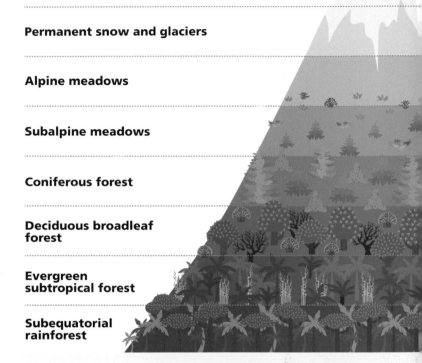

Permanent snow and glaciers

Alpine meadows

Subalpine meadows

Coniferous forest

Deciduous broadleaf forest

Evergreen subtropical forest

Subequatorial rainforest

**AFRICA
KILIMANJARO
19,341 FEET
(5,895 M)**

**OCEANIA
CARSTENSZ
PYRAMID
16,024 FEET
(4,884 M)**

Surviving harsh conditions

Moving across steep-sided mountains that are covered with small stones can be dangerous, so many mountain animals are both very agile and incredibly sure-footed. Mountain goats, such as the European chamois and ibex, are able to clamber up almost vertical slopes without slipping.

Temperatures can dip sharply as you climb up a mountain, so many mountain creatures, including llamas and snow leopards, have thick furry coats to keep them insulated.

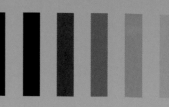

THE POLES

At the top and bottom of our planet are two icy habitats that experience long, dark winter periods where the Sun does not rise at all. But during the summer months, these places come alive as plants bloom and animals visit to rear their young.

Arctic tundra

To the south of the ice sheet that covers the Arctic is a region called the tundra. The soil below the surface is permanently frozen all year round, which stops large trees from growing and burrowing animals from digging deep underground to escape the harsh conditions. It also traps water on the surface, stopping it from draining away and forming swamps and lakes.

Visiting animals

In spring, warmer temperatures melt the top layer of soil, allowing flowers to bloom. Herds of reindeer and enormous flocks of birds arrive to breed and these attract predators and mosquitoes that feed on the blood of the visitors. When the temperatures drop again in autumn, these migrating animals head back south to avoid the worst of the cold.

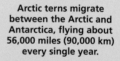

Arctic terns migrate between the Arctic and Antarctica, flying about 56,000 miles (90,000 km) every single year.

Arctic ice

There is no land around the North Pole and the sea is covered by a thick layer of ice throughout the year, although the amount of ice is declining as Earth's climate warms. Seals and walruses use the ice to rest while polar bears roam around the ice, hunting for prey.

Polar bear fur is translucent (almost see-through) and it looks white because it reflects visible light, camouflaging the animal against the ice and snow.

Arctic sea ice is declining at a rate of 13.1 percent every ten years. In 1979, the average amount of Arctic ice was 2.7 million square miles (7.05 million sq km). By 2020, this had declined to 1.51 million square miles (3.92 million sq km).

Antarctica

Antarctica is the windiest and coldest continent on the planet. Very few plants and animals can survive in the harsh habitat. Those that do are attracted by the rich seas during the summer months. Emperor penguins lay their eggs on the Antarctic ice and, while the mothers go back to the sea to feed and recover, the fathers look after the eggs and the newly hatched chicks, protecting them from the cold.

The lowest natural temperature recorded on Earth was

-128.6°F (-89.2°C),

which was measured at Vostok Station in Antarctica on July 21, 1983.

OCEAN HABITATS

The seas and oceans may cover about 71 percent of our planet, but we have explored very little of them. They contain an enormous range of habitats that range from teeming coral reefs to the inky blackness of the ocean depths.

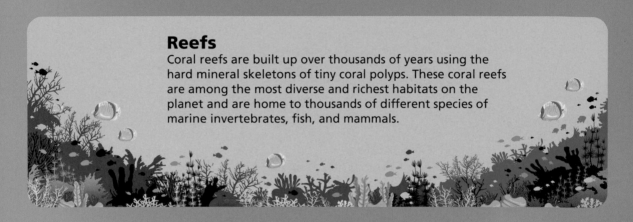

Reefs
Coral reefs are built up over thousands of years using the hard mineral skeletons of tiny coral polyps. These coral reefs are among the most diverse and richest habitats on the planet and are home to thousands of different species of marine invertebrates, fish, and mammals.

Plankton
The basis of ocean food chains are tiny floating phytoplankton. Using sunlight, they turn carbon dioxide and water into sugars in a process called photosynthesis. At times, numbers of these phytoplankton can increase so much that the blooms they create can be seen from space.

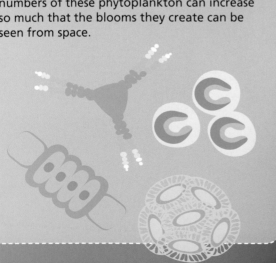

When phytoplankton do bloom, they attract larger creatures, including zooplankton and fish, to feed on them and any other sea creatures that are attracted to the area.

Seagrass and kelp

Found on the seafloor close to the coast, seagrass is a flowering plant that grows underwater. It provides a home to shellfish and other invertebrates and food for fish, mammals, such as manatees, and reptiles such as green turtles. Towering fronds of kelp, a type of algae, create thick underwater forests that provide shelter and food for sea creatures like shrimp and seals.

Deep sea and seafloor

Light fades rapidly as you plunge into the oceans, and below 660 feet (200 m) the water becomes darker until it is completely black by about 3,300 feet (1,000 m) down. Creatures living here are adapted to survive in these conditions and some of them even produce their own light to lure prey, scare off predators, or to communicate with each other.

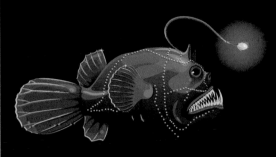

Deep-sea anglerfish have a light on the barbel above their heads which they wave around to attract prey toward their jaws.

The open ocean

Far out to sea, there are few nutrients to support much life and the open oceans have fewer living organisms than those areas closer to shore. Nutrients can well up from the deep in certain areas, such as those close to the continental shelf and, when that does occur, phytoplankton can thrive and bloom, attracting a whole host of other sea creatures to feed on them and the other animals lured by their presence.

ACCRETION

Adding material to something so that it increases in size. The early planets grew by attracting more rocks, dust, and gas to themselves by their gravitational force.

ADAPTATION

A feature that an organism has developed or inherited that makes it better suited to an environment.

ALBEDO

The amount of sunlight reflected by a surface. A bright, shiny surface, such as a mirror reflects a lot of sunlight, so it has a high albedo.

AMPLITUDE

The size of a wave, such as a sound wave or a shockwave from an earthquake. The bigger the wave, the higher the amplitude.

AQUIFER

An area of underground rock that holds a body of water.

ATMOSPHERE

The layer of gases that surrounds an object in space, such as a planet, or a moon.

AURORAE

The bands of glowing lights that form high above Earth as charged particles from the Sun interact with molecules in the atmosphere.

CLIMATE

The general weather conditions that a region experiences over a period of time.

CLIMATE CHANGE

The change in Earth's climate, in particular the rise in average temperatures across the planet caused by increased levels of greenhouse gases, such as carbon dioxide.

COMPACTION

Part of the process of forming sedimentary rock, when the rock particles are squeezed together by pressure from the layers of rock above them.

COMPOUNDS

A substance that is formed by two or elements.

CONVERGENT BOUNDARIES

A type of plate boundary where two tectonic plates are colliding with each other.

COPROLITES

Fossilised animal dung.

CORE

The region that lies at the very centre of a planet, moon or star.

CRUST

The outer layer of a planet or moon.

DIVERGENT BOUNDARIES

A type of plate boundary where two tectonic plates are pulling away from each other.

ECLIPSE

When one astronomical object passes in front of another, blocking out light from the Sun. A solar eclipse occurs when the Moon passes between Earth and the Sun, throwing a shadow on Earth's surface.

ELEMENT
A substance that is made up of only one type of atom. Elements include oxygen, lead, and carbon.

EPICENTRE
The point on Earth's surface directly above the source, or focus of an earthquake.

ERRATIC
A rock that is different from other rocks nearby and was dragged and placed there by a glacier.

EXOPLANET
A planet that orbits a star other than the Sun.

FOCUS
The site beneath Earth's surface where an earthquake originates.

GEYSER
A hole in the ground out of which steam and water that have been heated by volcanic activity shoot out under high pressure.

GLACIER
A large body of ice that moves very slowly.

GREENHOUSE GASES
The gases that cause the greenhouse effect, trapping the Sun's energy in Earth's atmosphere. Greenhouse gases include carbon dioxide and methane.

GROUNDWATER
Water that exists underground, either trapped in aquifers or moving very slowly downhill to empty into lakes and the sea.

HABITAT
The natural environment in which a plant or animal lives and develops.

HEADWARD EROSION
The erosion by a river or waterfall that lengthens a valley or gorge back towards the source of the river.

HOT SPOTS
Thin parts of crust found in the middle of a tectonic plate up through which molten rock can push to form volcanoes.

IGNEOUS ROCK
A type of rock that has been formed by molten rock cooling underground or on the surface.

INVERTEBRATE
An animal that does not have a backbone.

LAGOON
A body of water that is separated from the sea by a long line or bar of sand and rock.

LAHARS
Landslides of volcanic rock, mud, and water, that slide down the sides of a volcano, usually after heavy rain.

LAVA
Molten rock that has been thrown out onto Earth's surface during a volcanic eruption.

LONGSHORE DRIFT
The moving of sand and other beach debris along the coast that is caused by waves hitting the shore at an angle.

MAGMA
Molten rock beneath Earth's surface.

MAGNETOSPHERE
The region around a planet that is created by its magnetic field and affects any charged particles approaching the planet.

MANTLE
The region inside a moon or planet that lies between the core and the crust.

METAMORPHIC ROCK
A type of rock whose structure has been changed by extreme heat and/or pressure.

METEOR
A piece of rock that burn up in Earth's atmosphere.

METEORITE
A piece of rock that enters Earth's atmosphere and hits the surface.

MINERALS
A substance that forms naturally in Earth's rocks. Minerals include tin, iron, and salt.

ORBIT
The path of one object around another, such as the Moon's orbit around Earth.

PERMAFROST
A layer of rock and soil that is frozen all year.

PHOTOSYNTHESIS
The process by which plants use chlorophyll to turn sunlight, water and carbon dioxide into oxygen and sugars.

PHYTOPLANKTON
Tiny organisms that live in water and use photosynthesis to make sugars from which they can produce energy.

PLATE TECTONICS
The process by which the large plates of rock that make up Earth's crust move about and interact with each other.

PLATE BOUNDARIES
The regions between different tectonic plates.

PROTOPLANETS
Planets that are in the very early stages of their lives.

PYROCLASTIC FLOW
A cloud of super-hot gases, dust and rock that pour down the sides of a volcano during some eruptions, scorching everything in its path.

RADIOACTIVE
Something is radioactive when it releases radiation in the form of particles or energy.

RESPIRATION
The process by which living things use oxygen and sugars to produce carbon dioxide and water and release energy.

RUNOFF
Water that flows over the ground's surface.

SEDIMENTARY ROCK
A type of rock that is produced by the dropping and squeezing together of small rock particles.

SEDIMENTATION
When small pieces of rock, or sediment, are dropped to the bottom of a river, lake or the sea.

SEISMIC WAVES
The vibrations in the ground that are produced by an earthquake and spread out from the epicentre like ripples on a pond.

SOLAR SYSTEM
The Sun, as well as the eight planets and millions of smaller pieces of rock and ice that orbit around it.

SPIT
A long thin strip of land that sticks out into the sea.

STACK
A pillar of rock standing out in the sea that is the remains of a sea arch that has collapsed.

SUBDUCTION
When one tectonic plate is pushed beneath another and down into Earth's mantle.

SUPERCELL
A type of thunderstorm that is large and rotating and can create tornadoes.

SUPERVOLCANO
A huge type of volcano that can throw out more than 240 cubic miles (1,000 cubic kms) of lava, dust, gas, and other volcanic material.

TECTONIC PLATES
The large pieces of rock that Earth's crust is split up into. These tectonic plates move about, pulling apart, slamming into each other or rubbing against one another.

TRANSFORM BOUNDARIES
A type of plate boundary where two tectonic plates are rubbing against each other.

TRANSPIRATION
The evaporation of water from the leaves, stems or flowers of plants.

TROPICAL CYCLONE
A large rotating storm that forms over tropical waters and has winds that measure hundreds of miles per hour. They are also called hurricanes, typhoons or cyclones.

TSUNAMI
A very large wave that is triggered by an underwater earthquake or volcanic eruption. Tsunamis can travel thousands of miles and cause enormous amounts of damage on the other side of an ocean from their source.

TUNDRA
The regions around the poles and high up on mountains where the ground below the surface is frozen all year round, preventing trees from growing.

UPHEAVAL
In geology, this is the process by which a piece of rock is pushed up towards the surface. It is also known as uplift.

VOLCANIC BOMB
A large piece of rock that is thrown out by a volcanic eruption and slams into the ground with an explosive force.

ZOOPLANKTON
Tiny sea creatures that are usually made up of small shellfish and the young of fish.

INDEX

ACKNOWLEDGMENTS

Picture Credits

FC-front cover, BC-back cover, t-top, b-bottom, l-left,r-right, c-centre

All images Shutterstock.com unless stated.

6br TaLyDes, 7 BlueRingMedia, 8 Mopic, 9 Vectomart, 13b Diego Barucco, 15br Vector Tradition, 16b Natali Snailcat, 17t Pablo Prat, 17b REANEW, 18-19t Lisitsa, 18b, 19 Alhovik, 20-21 Kolonko, 22 Designua, 23t NTL studio, 23bl Peter Hermes Furian, 23br fredrisher, 24 Den Zorin, 25cr VectorShow, 25b GoodStudio, 26-27b Vlasov_38RUS, 30-31 trgrowth, 30br Rvector, 32-33t VectorMine, 33tr Fouad A. Saad, 32-33b trgrowth, 34tr Vector Tradition, 34-35b Designua, 35t Porcupen, 37b EreborMountain, 38 Designua, 38-39 Nsit, 41br Agil Leonardo, 42bl Tatsiana Tsyhanova, 42r Amanita Silvicora, 43b HappyPictures, 44 SaveJungle, 45tl BSVIT, 45tr laverock, 45br Walnut Bird, 46-47 Kavic.C, 48 MicroOne, 49t astudio, 49b VectorMine, 51 Kavic.C, 52-53 stihii, 53tr Panda Vector, 53bl La Gorda, 53br Arctium Lappa, 54b, 55tl, 55bl Kavic.C, 55r lady-luck, 56tl jkcDesign, 56tc BlueRingMedia, 56cr toshkastock, 57tl newelle, 57tr Tancha, 57bl jagoda, 58b NeutronStar8, 59t Hennadii H, 59bl Blue bee, 59br suriyo tataisong, 60 ActiveLines, 61tl Magicleaf, 61tc Amanita Silvicora, 61tr MicroOne, 61b Spreadthesign, 62-63 Oceloti, 62bl Anatolir, 64-65 zombiu26, 65tr Tetreb88, 65cr moj0j0, 65br GoodStudio, 68bl KittyVector, 68br curiosity, 69b Nasky, 70bl Alfmaler, 70-71 zombiu26, 71tr Nenilkime, 72-73 VectorMine, 75t wickerwood, 75b Art Berry, 77br Sentavio, 78-79 zombiu26, 81b Amadeu Blasco, 82-83 BigMouse, 83t StockSmartStart, 83b wickerwood, 84 MarySan, 85tl Sudowoodo, 85tr VectorShow, 85b, 86-87 Macrovector, 88tr Sunny_nsk, 88cl ByEmo, 88br Anna.zabella, 89tl Svetla, 89bl kuroksta, 89br MarySan, 91br humanart, 92t BlueRingMedia, 92b K3Star, 93t vectortatu, 93c ActiveLines, 93b AnnstasAg, 94-95 Natali Snailcat, 94c Alfmaler, 95tl Pandum, 95tc Alhovik, 95tr VikiVector, 96l MarBom, 96-97 fluidworkshop, 98 Colin Hayes, 99br m. malinika, 102-103 GraphicsRF.com, 103br Sarema, 104, 105 J. Marini, 105cr Natali Snailcat, 106 ActiveLines, 107tr zombiu26, 107bl OK-SANA, 107br A7880S, 108t Zvereva Yana, 108b Lidiia, 109tl Ara Hovhannisyan, 109tr Hennadii H, 110-111 BlueRingMedia, 111tl WPAINTER-Std, 111cr Kirill Kalchenko, 111br kareemov1000, 112-113 adisetia, 112tr Annari, 113tl BlueRingMedia, 113tr Adazhiy Dmytro, 113cr Shanvood, 115tr alinabel, 115b Rhoeo, 116cr serkan mutan, 116b, 117t AnnstasAg, 117b AQ_taro_neo, 118t Natali Snailcat, 118bl WhiteDragon, 119tl suriyo tataisong, 119tr Bourbon-88, 118-119b irkus